busy WITH
buttons

save, stitch, create and share

JILL GORSKI

OHIO

mycraftivity.com
Connect. Create. Explore.

Busy With Buttons: Save, Stitch, Create and Share. Copyright ©
2009 by Jill Gorski. Manufactured in China. All rights reserved. The patterns and drawings in this book are for the personal use of the reader.
By permission of the author and publisher, they may be either hand-
traced or photocopied to make single copies, but under no circum-
stances may they be resold or republished. No other part of this book
may be reproduced in any form or by any electronic or mechanical
means including information storage and retrieval systems without
permission in writing from the publisher, except by a reviewer who

 may quote brief passages in a review. Published by Krause
Publications, an imprint of F+W Media, Inc., 4700 East
Galbraith Road, Cincinnati, Ohio, 45236. (800) 289-0963.
First edition.

Other fine Krause Publications titles are available from your local
bookstore, craft supply store or online retailer, or visit our website
at www.fwmedia.com.

13 12 11 10 09   5 4 3 2 1

DISTRIBUTED IN CANADA BY FRASER DIRECT
100 Armstrong Avenue
Georgetown, ON, Canada L7G 5S4
Tel: (905) 877-4411

DISTRIBUTED IN THE U.K. AND EUROPE BY DAVID & CHARLES
Brunel House, Newton Abbot, Devon, TQ12 4PU, England
Tel: (+44) 1626 323200
Fax: (+44) 1626 323319
Email: postmaster@davidandcharles.co.uk

DISTRIBUTED IN AUSTRALIA BY CAPRICORN LINK
P.O. Box 704, S. Windsor NSW, 2756 Australia
Tel: (02) 4577-3555

Library of Congress Cataloging in Publication Data
Gorski, Jill.
   Busy with buttons : save, stitch, create, and share / Jill Gorski.
      p. cm.
   Includes bibliographical references and index.
   ISBN-13: 978-0-89689-732-8 (pbk. : alk. paper)
   ISBN-10: 0-89689-732-X (pbk. : alk. paper)
   1. Button craft. I. Title.
   TT880.G67 2009
   745.58'4--dc22
                        2009015998

Edited by Stefanie Laufersweiler
Designed by Julie Barnett
Production coordinated by Matthew Wagner
Photography by David Peterson
Photos on pages 16-17 by Kris Kandler
Photo styling by Jan Nickum
Illustrations by Hayes Shanesy

ABOUT THE AUTHOR

Jill Gorski grew up in Lakewood, California, surrounded
by a large family of crafters and sewers. Her maternal
great-grandmother made lovely quilts, and both of her
grandmothers embroidered, crocheted and sewed. Jill's
mother made beautiful clothes for her five children
to wear. Jill learned many different skills from these
talented women. She made many of her own clothes,
and clothes for her own children. She especially enjoys
doing handwork, including smocking and embroidery.

   In 1993, Jill's husband, Steve, took a
job in Tucson, Arizona, and it was
there that she learned to quilt.
She never dreamed that from
this would come a passion
for something so seemingly
unrelated, and yet so inter-
twined with everything else
she enjoys: buttons. At first
she only wanted to make a few
button bracelets as gifts. A life-
changing moment came for her when
her dear friend Linda told her, "If it doesn't move, put a
button on it," and Jill decided it didn't matter if it moved
or not! Soon she was making button crafts of all kinds.
Jill is now a member of the National Button Society, the
Colorado State Button Society and the Colorado Springs
Button Club.

   Jill and Steve currently live in Colorado Springs, Colorado. They travel quite a bit with Jill's business, Jillions of
Buttons (jillionsofbuttons.com), as well as taking trips
to see their three children, Chad, Bryan and Emily, all
of whom serve in the United States' armed forces. Jill is
also the author of the comprehensive reference book
Warman's® Buttons Field Guide (2009).

METRIC CONVERSION CHART

to convert	to	multiply by
inches	centimeters	2.54
centimeters	inches	0.4
feet	centimeters	30.5
centimeters	feet	0.03
yards	meters	0.9
meters	yards	1.1

DEDICATION ~ *I lovingly dedicate this book to the women in my life who passed on to me their love for their family through their sewing skills, especially my grandmothers, Georgia McCormick McDowell ("Gramma") and Genevieve Mass Snedden ("Nanny").*

My Nanny's robe buttons: the most prized buttons in my entire collection. They may be plastic and plain and not extraordinarily pretty, but their value is priceless to me.

acknowledgments

This book came to be as a result of a loving family, dear friends and patience from all who know me.

❀ Thanks to my husband, Steve, for doing it all, especially when you really didn't feel like it. I couldn't have done this book without your support, Bear. I love you!

❀ To my children, Chad, Bryan and Emily, and their spouses, Anna and Lisa. Thanks for listening, even when you had heard it all before.

❀ To my Mama, Janet Hayes, for your love, support and labors. I really love being able to share this with you. Thanks also to "Turkey" for your help while Mama "goes off to play" with me and for helping at shows.

❀ To my sister (in-law, but I've never thought so), Jeannine, who never stops encouraging, helping and thinking of me. I'm glad I could be the one to show you and the kids new "vices" (sorry, Jay!).

❀ To my "FedUp sister," Linda Powell, who taught me to look at everything with different eyes and who has always encouraged my daydreams.

❀ To my friends Joan Johnson-Porter and Carolyn McCormick. This book would never have come to life without you! I am forever grateful for your lessons and friendship.

❀ To acquisitions editor Candy Wiza at F+W Media for sticking with me and believing in my dream; to editor Stefanie Laufersweiler for picking up the pieces and really listening to me; and also to the staff at F+W for their support.

❀ A special thanks to my brother Jay for constructing the Handy Notions Holder, as well as for all your help and love.

❀ Sincere thanks go to Linda Schwarz and Sharon Schlotzhauer of the Piecing Partners Quilt Guild for coming to my rescue and lending their incredible quilting talents to my projects.

So many others have been there for me along the way and I wish I could name all of you. I hope that I have told each of you in person how much you mean to me. God bless you all.

contents

Introduction ~ 6

Collecting Buttons ~ 8

Sorting Your Stash ~ 12

Cleaning, Care and Identification ~ 14

Quick-Reference Button Guide ~ 16

Choosing the Right Buttons for a Project ~ 18

Button Attachment Techniques ~ 20

4

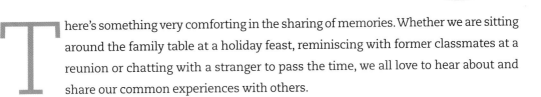

There's something very comforting in the sharing of memories. Whether we are sitting around the family table at a holiday feast, reminiscing with former classmates at a reunion or chatting with a stranger to pass the time, we all love to hear about and share our common experiences with others.

This book came about after I listened to countless people share their stories of the family button box: the buttons they've collected over the years or that have been passed down to them from previous generations. While details may have differed, the smiles on their faces and the tugs at their heartstrings told me what I already knew: buttons are a loving reminder of shared family time and lessons learned that last a lifetime.

My mission in writing this book is to reintroduce you to your family buttons (or help acquaint you with someone else's collection that has lost its family) and remind you of the treasures that lie buried in your box, tin, jar or sewing basket. I believe that these buttons have stories to tell, and I hope to help you speak their language and share those stories with others. Most of us would not keep family heirlooms locked away and hidden in some damp, dark place. Rather, we proudly display them in our homes, giving them special attention, care and places of honor. The projects in this book are designed to help you find those places to show your buttons in decorative and practical ways and smile as you look at them, just as you would a favorite quilt or photograph.

Some of you may simply have spare buttons you want to do something creative with. For you, I hope this book is not merely an idea giver but the first step in an unexpectedly delightful journey in button collecting. As my own journey led me to start collecting jars, bags and boxes of buttons at thrift stores and flea markets and from my friends, I took the liberty of assigning stories to them and their former owners. My curiosity began to get the better of me, however, and soon I was reading everything I could find related to buttons. One of the first books I discovered was a children's book by Peter and Connie Roop, called *Buttons for General Washington*, an intriguing story about a patriotic family who used buttons to help smuggle encrypted messages to General Washington's troops. Further reading revealed more stories about buttons connected to and entwined with history. How exciting to imagine the stories linked to the buttons in my possession!

Fancy or plain, large or small, all buttons are wonderful. I hope that after reading this book, you will never look at a button the same way again.

Collecting Buttons

Humans, by their very nature, tend to be collectors. There are many theories as to why this is so. It could be the prehistoric hunter-gatherer that is innate in all of us. We may collect things as a way of defining ourselves by what we have or do. Another theory suggests that who we are is structured by where we come from and where we belong, therefore we crave things from our past. Regardless of the reason, there is no doubt in my mind that being a collector is just plain fun.

Buttons have been collected for centuries. As early as the twelfth century, jeweled sets of buttons were created

These charming plastic buttons are from the early 1900s. Some, such as the circus lion and the carrots, originally were part of a set; others, such as the Ritz cracker, are one of a kind. Who can resist collecting these fun reminders of days gone by?

for and coveted by royalty and the aristocracy as a way to show wealth and power. Buttons have been found listed among household inventories and in wills to be passed on to future generations.

By refusing to import buttons from Europe, a young nation once encouraged its citizens to craft and wear "American-made" buttons to demonstrate their solidarity and independence. General George Washington, who loathed ostentatious displays, agreed to wear a set of fine metal buttons bearing his initials on his coat for his presidential inauguration. These buttons are among the most collectible and coveted buttons today.

Male soldiers—in fact, men in general—were the first collectors of buttons, exchanging uniform buttons on the battlefield. It is, indeed, a testament to the humble button that, even during a time of great economic depression in the United States, collecting buttons became an organized activity.

In 1938, Gertrude Patterson spoke to the nation on a radio program for collectors of all kinds about her passion for buttons. Soon afterward, the National Button Society (NBS) was founded and button collectors were able to share their buttons, stories and enthusiasm for these tiny gems. Today the NBS, thirty-nine state button societies and hundreds of local button clubs promote educational research, documenting the findings of this research and "the preservation of the aesthetic and historical significance of buttons for future generations."

Building Your Collection

Buttons continue to be a popular collectible today, due in part to their affordability. Most twentieth-century buttons can be purchased for under five dollars each. Even the most coveted buttons from this era can often be purchased for less than twenty dollars. I am often asked what the most expensive button in my collection is worth. I have paid up to

These modern (post-World War II) glass buttons were made in West Germany. Even though all are striped, the construction of those stripes varies from button to button. Here we see moonglows (in which a thin layer of clear glass is applied over the color layer), colored stripes on colored bodies, colored stripes on white bodies, gold luster, design under glass, satin glass and candy stripes.

gained more knowledge and confidence, I increased my budget slightly to include some finer buttons in my collection.

Another school of thought would be to spend a little more for specific buttons and acquire fewer, but finer, buttons. Many people concentrate on collecting buttons that illustrate a particular theme, such as dogs, or that are made of a certain button material, such as glass. In fact, buttons can augment another collection (for example, you might add bear buttons to your stuffed bear collection). My best advice is to collect what appeals to you and don't worry about what's popular.

Another reason buttons are a popular collectible is that they are plentiful and relatively easy to find. My search for great buttons began at flea markets, thrift stores and yard sales. In addition, I let everyone—and I do mean *everyone*—know that

seventy-five dollars for a single button—a trifle compared to some serious collectors and competitors—but my favorite buttons are not worth ten cents to anyone else, yet they are priceless to me. Your collection does not need to be expensive to be comprehensive as well as fun.

As a new button collector with few buttons of my own, I decided to set a dollar limit for myself of five dollars for a jar of buttons, and one dollar for a single button. I managed to amass a sizable collection of buttons in a very short time. As I

Buttons with realistic subjects, such as these glass ones depicting women's faces (circa 1930), were all the rage from 1930 to 1950. They depicted many popular items of the time, including cigarettes, cocktails and sporting activities. They were made from glass, Bakelite and plastic, often in themed sets.

Even if you collect something other than buttons, you might want to add buttons to your existing collection. Buttons can be found depicting any subject you can imagine—crowns, for instance—and so they can become a secondary collectible for your favorite collection.

Buildings and scenes—some recognizable, others representative—are a popular subject on buttons. The *mother-daughter pair* here—a large and small version of the same design—shows a mounted figure riding toward a castle gate in a design entitled, "The Prince Returns." The elaborate heart border lends an elegant look. The pewter button at the top left, depicting a Tyrolean scene, was manufactured by the Battersea Company and is so marked and dated (1976) on the back.

Button subjects were often reproduced in a variety of materials. Sometimes a manufacturer would copy a competitor's designs, but often designs were just so popular that they were reissued in later years. This leaf-and-berry design, shown in metal and plastic versions, is a good example. Variations on the same theme have been found in several other materials, sizes and finishes.

I wanted buttons. My next (and best) move was to attend a button show sponsored by my state button society. It was there that I found affordable, collectible buttons for purchase, educational seminars and information about buttons, and new friends who gave freely of their time, talents and even their buttons.

I quickly learned how to identify common button materials with the use of a good magnifying glass, a magnet, and most importantly, my senses of smell, touch, sight and hearing. I also found that the back of a button holds far more information about its origin than does the front. And, as I too discovered, how to properly store your buttons is perhaps the most critical piece of information you will need as you grow your collection.

The most important thing to remember with button collecting is that there are levels for everyone and every size of collection. It does not need to be an all-consuming hobby, but the more you learn about it, the easier it may become to get drawn into the sheer fun of it. For me, it all started with a love for sewing and history (mine and that of the world). I have always been intrigued by the way everything in life, though seemingly disconnected, is so entwined. I hope you find your passion in or through your buttons.

Sometimes called *cut steels*, these metal buttons have faceted steel rivet embellishments. Shown are a dragon, a sailing ship (with a mother-of-pearl ring), a rooster head and a mask representing Sol, the sun god. All are nineteenth-century buttons, yet still very affordable (less than twenty dollars).

Twinkle buttons are made of metal and have pierced tops that reveal a shiny liner inside. They come in many shapes and sizes; the liners also come in a variety of colors. These buttons were the "bling" of their day!

Grandma's Button Box

My grandma saved so many things
She thought that she might need
Like rubber bands and bits of foil
"Waste not" was her creed!

Now thanks to her I have this box
That's full as it can be
Of lovely little buttons
Such precious memories!

These brass ones once were shiny
But not so anymore
They come from all the uniforms
Our family proudly wore!

Here's a shiny glass one
From her favorite dress of blue
And tiny pearls from my dress
That she made when I was two!

These white ones are just plain and round
From pj's Grandpa wore
Until they got so paper thin
And the fabric finally tore!

My favorite one is yellow
Not really much to see
But it's from her robe she used to wear
When she would read to me!

Just look at all these buttons!
Our family's history!
My grandma saved them in this box
Oh lucky, lucky me!

~ JILL GORSKI ~

Sorting Your Stash

When most of us think of a button, we picture a small, round, four-holed shirt button. While it's true you will find many plastic shirt buttons in your button box, I am fairly certain that you will also find buttons that are not so familiar to you. It is critical that you know what materials your buttons are made from in order to clean, store and successfully use them on projects.

A tin full of buttons can be overwhelming, so I encourage you to assess what you have by sorting your buttons. How to sort buttons is a common discussion topic among collectors, and we all have our own methods. Eventually you will find a way that works best for you; for now, I will share with you my sorting method.

First, place a dish towel in a cookie sheet or cake pan and carefully pour the contents of the box into this initial container for easier viewing. Be aware that you will find more than buttons in your box! I have been stuck more than once by needles, screws,

These small, glass "kiddie" buttons from the 1930s and '40s were marketed for children's wear. They depict cute animals and children.

pins and other sharp objects. Occasionally I have discovered fun objects mixed in, such as tax tokens (which prompted an Internet search and history lesson), thimbles and keys.

Next, find containers to sort your buttons into. Muffin tins, bowls, plastic meat trays and the like all work well. Consider using paper bowls, muffin cup liners or coffee filters to not only help you lift out your buttons easily but also to protect them from chipping or breaking.

Start by sorting into broad groupings, then divide those groups into smaller, more specific ones later. I usually begin by sorting according to material: metal, plastic, pearl and shell, glass and vegetable ivory.

A small portion of my collection of green glass buttons. You could specialize in one color or style of glass button and amass a very large yet affordable collection.

These china buttons with stencil designs (circa 1840) were manufactured in France, England and Long Island, New York, for use on undergarments, shirts and dresses. Due to their small size and sturdy construction, they were common on clothing for the working class. Nearly sixty stencil patterns have been cataloged. Another style of china button is decorated with calico designs that were made to match fabrics of the day; over 325 patterns have been noted. Many collectors strive to have one of every known design and size—a daunting task!

You might have a miscellaneous bowl as well for, say, fabric and upholstery-type buttons, or buttons that don't fit into the other groups. If you are not certain what kind of material your button is made from, that's OK; give it your best initial guess. As you learn more about button identification, you can sort your buttons more accurately later.

Which buttons to keep and which to throw out is certainly up to you. You will undoubtedly find buttons that are *crazing* (cracking), broken, rusted, dulled or discolored. Separate these "sick" buttons from your healthy ones. Some will be beyond repair and can be thrown out. If you wish, you can use the others to help you learn more about button construction and to practice repair and cleaning.

Vegetable ivory whistle buttons have one hole on top and two holes on the back. This same whistle construction style is also found in plastic, glass and shell buttons, among others.

Cleaning, Care and Identification

Tools of the trade, from left to right: an awl, magnet, magnifying glass and plastic-coated wire.

back, as opposed to sew-through buttons—is to store your buttons on cards you can cut from acid-free mat board, available at framing or craft stores. Punch holes in the board with an awl or ice pick, place the shanks of your buttons in the holes, and secure the buttons to the board with plastic-coated wire. (I do not recommend pipe cleaners, as the wire is exposed to moisture and can rust.) Store your carded buttons in a pretty box or file cabinet. Other fun storage options are candy dishes or candle holders that encourage people to play with your buttons—something I definitely endorse!

✿ **The backs of your buttons contain a plethora of information.** The type of shank, backmarks (manufacturer's name and possibly location) and material characteristics, such as grain lines, color and pick marks—a tiny hole in the back of a horn button, made

Here are some overall guidelines that apply to most buttons:

✿ *Never* **clean your buttons by immersing them in water.** New plastic buttons and some shell buttons are the exception, but even these buttons have a better alternative for cleaning (see pages 16-17). Keeping your buttons dry, free from rust and mold, is imperative.

✿ **Many buttons are made from natural materials and therefore need to breathe.** So, airtight storage containers are not recommended. If your buttons came in a box, returning them to their original box is fine for some (but not all) of your buttons, as long as the top is left on loosely or has holes in it. If you must keep your collection in a tin or jar, leave the lid off. A better storage system, particularly for shank buttons—those with a loop on the

My favorite button-cleaning tools are simple: a jewelry polishing cloth and a child's soft toothbrush. Other useful items are mineral oil and a clean, soft cloth (such as an old T-shirt) for applying it.

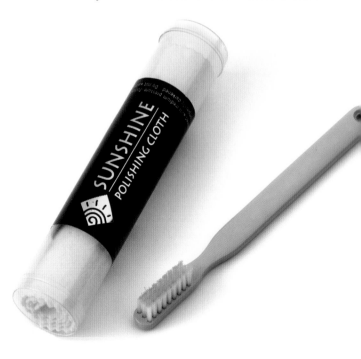

These celluloid buttons, topped with thin sheets of celluloid and backed with metal, date from about the 1920s. Three display *tight-top* construction, while the one with the triangle is a *glow bubble*. Invented in 1870, celluloid was avoided by button makers after its extreme flammability was discovered. Never put a celluloid button near an iron or in a dryer! Also, keep them away from other buttons because they release toxic gases if they decompose (see page 17).

when the button was removed from its manufacturing mold with a small pick—can provide clues to help you identify your buttons, so flip those buttons over.

The quick-reference guide on pages 16-17 will give you tips on identifying, cleaning and caring for specific types of buttons. It is by no means all-inclusive, but it covers most of the typical buttons you will come across. For more detailed information and additional button types, consult the Resources section on page 126 for available guidebooks, websites and organizations.

Knowing what material your buttons are made from will help you to preserve your treasure. In addition, you will be able to choose the buttons that are best suited to the projects. For example, if your finished project will be washed, you need to be certain that the buttons you select are washable.

Pictorial or picture buttons depict popular subjects of their day: the Queen Mary (celluloid), Elsie the Borden Cow (plastic) and "Yum-Yum" from the Gilbert and Sullivan opera *The Mikado* (brass). Buttons often can be dated and identified by their subjects, but this method is not foolproof. Subjects were often reissued, or manufactured as reproductions. The material the buttons are made from provides a more reliable way to date them.

Dogs have long been a popular subject for buttons. These two buttons from the late nineteenth century are brass applied to steel backgrounds. The one on the left is, I believe, called "In the Doghouse," while the smaller button on the right shows a terrier's head. Handle steel buttons with a magnetic tool rather than your fingers, because the salts and oils from your skin can tarnish them.

Buttons were sometimes used to advertise. This is one of my favorites because my grandfather owned a service station and my father worked as a parts manager for car dealerships all my life. It reads: "When you button up your overcoat ... Remember your car. Change to Alemite Temprite winter gear lubricant." This button was produced as a promotional giveaway in 1937 and would sell today for about ten dollars.

QUICK-REFERENCE BUTTON GUIDE

TYPE/MATERIAL	IDENTIFICATION TIPS/FACTS	CLEANING/CARE
GLASS	Feels cool to the touch and slightly weighty in your hand. Tap the button on your tooth and you will hear a very distinctive clicking sound.	Clean with a slightly damp cloth if the button has no paint or luster. If it does, simply polish with a clean, dry cloth, being careful not to remove decorative paints and finishes.
SHELL and PEARL	All pearl buttons are shell, but not all shell buttons are pearl. Many shell buttons are thin and fragile. The back of the button often has the outer "bark" of the shell still visible and may reveal what type of shell button you have.	Gently clean shell buttons with a child's soft toothbrush and water if very dirty. Otherwise, just use a clean polishing cloth. If the buttons have lost their luster, rub on a touch of mineral oil, then wipe with a clean cloth, ensuring the buttons are dry.
VEGETABLE IVORY	Vegetable ivory comes from the meat of a nut and has a lovely cream color. Because the material is dense, only the top layer accepts dye. Look at the back of the button and you will see the cream color where the button's shank has been drilled through (see photo on page 18).	These buttons are sensitive to moisture, so never use water to clean them, only a clean polishing cloth.
METAL	This is a broad term for a number of specific materials, and buttons have been made from many types. Steel buttons will be attracted to a magnet. Brass buttons are famous for *greening*, discoloration caused by exposure to moisture over time.	In general, never use water to clean metal buttons (steel ones are particularly susceptible to rusting). Instead, use a child's soft toothbrush and a polishing cloth. To combat stubborn greening damage, try applying vinegar with a cotton swab, then let the buttons dry thoroughly in the sun. Store them separately from other buttons.
FABRIC	As fabrics age, the fibers become very brittle, so handle these buttons carefully.	Fabric buttons typically have a metal or wooden form under them that water could ruin, depending on the age of your button. A gentle dusting is the best treatment for these buttons.
CHINA and PORCELAIN	China buttons can be identified by looking at their backs; very often you will see an area in the center that looks rough or sandy, where the button rested during firing. China buttons were commonly decorated with either a stenciled design or a patterned design that replicated calico fabrics of the day.	These buttons may be cleaned with water, if you are careful not to remove the designs in the process. A clean, dry cloth often is all that's needed.
BONE and HORN	These natural materials often show their cell structure. Horn buttons appear transparent, especially around the outer edges, when held up to a light source.	Never use water on these buttons. A clean cloth works well, and a dab of mineral oil can brighten and restore luster.

TYPE/MATERIAL	IDENTIFICATION TIPS/FACTS	CLEANING/CARE
LEATHER	Leather can be made from a variety of animal skins including cow, alligator and even shark. Leather buttons are often made over a metal or wooden form.	If your leather buttons have any mold on them, it is wise to discard them. A soft toothbrush can clean crevices and a polishing cloth will do the rest.
CELLULOID	Celluloid is made from natural plant materials and chemicals. Celluloid buttons have very distinctive shanks: one type is fairly thick, clear plastic in the shape of the Greek letter omega; the other type is thinner, domed and resembles a toy train tunnel.	Clean with a polishing cloth. Be careful not to rub too hard, as the dyes used for these buttons were not always stable. When the plant materials that make up the celluloid decompose, chemical gases are released that can destroy other buttons if they share the same airtight container. Store celluloid buttons separately from other buttons.
BAKELITE	Bakelite, the first true plastic introduced in the early 1900s, turns a lovely warm yellow as it ages. Some buttons made from Bakelite were dyed in browns, greens and reds. Because Bakelite is very collectible and commands a higher price, proper testing is key. One test: Rub the button with your finger until warm; there should be a distinctive odor of formaldehyde. Or, wet a cotton swab with Scrubbing Bubbles Bathroom Cleaner and gently rub the back of the button. If the swab turns yellow, your button is Bakelite. This method will not damage your buttons.	Clean these buttons carefully, as Bakelite has a very thin layer of finish that you don't want to remove. Use a damp cloth and a very gentle dish soap if needed.
PLASTICS (old and new)	Plastic buttons are plentiful, and many older plastic buttons from the 1930s and '40s are especially fun to collect because they were made in all kinds of shapes and sometimes came in sets.	A damp cloth will clean most plastic buttons. Clean very dirty ones with warm, soapy water and a soft toothbrush.
WOOD	Most wooden buttons are plainly designed, but easy to identify by their grain lines. Older buttons can be found that are of metal design with a wood background.	Never use water to clean a wooden button. A soft cloth is best, with a dab of furniture oil or polish. Be sure the button is thoroughly dry before storing it.
RUBBER front back	These may look like plain brown or black buttons until you spot the identifying marks on the back, which include the Goodyear name (usually), patent date and manufacturer (the letters "I.R.C.Co." indicate the button shown was made by the India Rubber Comb Company, of New York). Indeed, the same formula used to make tires was adapted to make buttons. Many U.S. Navy uniform buttons were made from rubber.	Avoid soap and water when cleaning rubber. A clean polishing cloth works best, but a dab of baby oil (allowed to dry thoroughly) will add a shine.

Choosing the Right Buttons for a Project

The projects in this book are designed to showcase your buttons to their best advantage. Remember, though, that a successful project will, more often than not, begin with the button. So many times I've heard others say they are seeking the perfect button for a particular project and they search forever, often settling for a button that merely "works." Avoid this frustration by choosing the buttons you want to work with first, then deciding which project would best suit them. Let the buttons "speak" to you rather than launching a time-consuming and potentially disappointing search for the perfect button for a project.

Other times, you will spot opportunities for buttons to be the crowning detail on a project. Most of us have items around the house that could use a little extra something. There's that tote bag that's a great size, but not very exciting to look at. Maybe it's a lackluster pillow or shirt. Blank

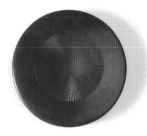

Vegetable ivory buttons were made between 1850 and 1940 from the nut meat of the tagua or corozo palm that grows in South America. The nut is sliced, shaped, dyed and decorated. Because the dye does not easily penetrate the dense material, you can see the natural color of the nut where the shank was drilled through on the back of the button. These buttons become cracked or crazed when exposed to too much moisture, so do not use them for items that will be frequently laundered.

canvases are everywhere if you look for them! Don't limit yourself. Look for places that could use a special touch and ask yourself, "Where can I put a button on this?"

Whether you are personalizing a ready-made garment or planning a creation of your own design, a little planning will go a long way toward success. When it is required of them, buttons should be functional as well as beautiful, so it is critical to choose the correct button for the job—as well as the best method for attaching the button.

Also consider:

❖ **The material of both the button and the project.** Will the fabric you plan to use need to be washed or dry cleaned periodically? Many types of buttons cannot be soaked in water. Many delicate buttons, such as those containing rhinestones, can't be dry cleaned. Is the project fabric lightweight or delicate? Your buttons should not be so large or heavy that they pull on the fabric. Is your fabric heavy and thick? Your buttons should be substantial enough to hold the fabric together.

❖ **The shape of the button.** Buttons come in lots of great novelty shapes and designs, and they really can be

BUILD A BETTER BUTTONHOLE

- Determine the correct size for a buttonhole by measuring the perimeter of the button, dividing that number in half, then adding 1/16" (2mm).

- Always use a seam sealant, such as Dritz Fray Check, on your buttonholes to strengthen them. Let them dry completely prior to cutting them open.

- Your button should slide through the buttonhole with ease but not slack.

- Sew a small square of stabilizer to the underside of the garment where the button attaches to lessen the stress on the button and prevent pulling, tearing or sagging.

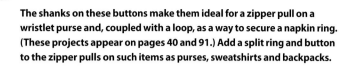

The shanks on these buttons make them ideal for a zipper pull on a wristlet purse and, coupled with a loop, as a way to secure a napkin ring. (These projects appear on pages 40 and 91.) Add a split ring and button to the zipper pulls on such items as purses, sweatshirts and backpacks.

like icing on a cake! Besides appearance, however, some thought should be given to whether your project requires buttonholes, or if the buttons are needed to hold something securely. A conventional buttonhole often will not work for a novelty button. A ball-shaped button may not securely hold a tight-fitting blouse together.

✿ **The size of both the button and the buttonhole.** Many people try in vain to replace a button lost from a garment with a perfect match. If you don't care for the existing buttons, though, this is a great excuse to change them all. But say you find these fabulous buttons, but they are a fraction too big or too small for the buttonholes on the garment. Not to worry! You can make a buttonhole bigger by reinforcing the existing hole and slightly enlarging it at the same time. First, place a piece of interfacing slightly larger than your desired buttonhole under the existing buttonhole. Then satin stitch over the buttonhole and extend the length when you come to the end. Complete the stitching, apply seam sealant and re-cut the opening once the sealant is dry. To make a buttonhole smaller, stitch one end closed with a wide satin stitch. You might even sew the holes shut, cover them with decorative fabric patches and resew new buttonholes. This technique works great for torn buttonholes as well.

At first glance, the buttons lining the top edge of this box look identical, but they're not. Nearly each one is different from the next, but they work well together here to define the edges of the lid because they are similar in size and color.

Button Attachment Techniques

Above all, it is important to know how to sew on a button correctly. Even if you don't gravitate toward craft projects that require it, it's a practical skill that won't go to waste.

Always use a good-quality thread. Polyester topstitching thread is strong and doesn't fray, making it a solid choice for thick or large buttons and shank buttons. This kind of thread can be unattractive, however, when used with a smaller or delicate button. In this case, double a regular sewing-weight thread, knotting the ends together.

Start sewing under the spot where the sew-through button will go. Place a pin or toothpick that matches the thickness of your fabric between the fabric and the button. For example, if you are sewing a button onto a silk blouse, you need only a small pin, but you will need a toothpick (or two) for a wool jacket. Sew the button on by passing the thread through the holes three to four times. Wrap the thread on the needle around the threads where the toothpick is, in a figure eight. This creates a short *thread shank* that helps the button fit properly when buttoned. A shank button can be sewn directly in place, as the shank functions in the same way as the thread shank.

Bring the thread to the back and knot it securely. Lastly, use a drop of seam sealant on the knot. Once it dries, your button will be secure.

Most sewing machines, old and new, offer a button-attaching foot if you'd rather skip the handwork.

Attachment Alternatives

Here are several other ways to attach your buttons so you can use them to their ultimate potential.

✿ **Tie one on.** Use a decorative thread such as perle cotton or embroidery floss to tie buttons onto a project. Sew from the front of the button to the back, and up through another hole to the top again. Cut, leaving tails of thread. Tie a square knot, then secure with a drop of seam sealant. You can fray the ends of the floss, or let them hang long or short.

An alternative to sewing buttons on is tying them on with decorative thread.

✿ **Attach decorative buttons to backer buttons.** When you want to add large, decorative buttons to an existing item with small buttonholes, or if you aren't sure whether the fabric in a new project can handle the stress of large buttonholes, try using backer buttons. These work much like cuff links in French cuffs. Normally, a button is sewn to the back fabric and is buttoned through a buttonhole in the front fabric. With the backer-button method, a second small buttonhole is created in the back fabric directly behind the buttonhole in the front fabric. The decorative button is not sewn to the fabric at all, but to a small, sturdy backer button. The backer button is then buttoned through both fabric layers from front to back, leaving only the decorative button showing in front. (When sewing the buttons together, make sure the thread shank between them is long enough to accommodate both fabric layers.) One advantage to this method is that, like cuff links, the buttons can be removed very easily, so it works well for delicate buttons on items that require regular cleaning.

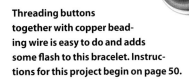

Get the **"buttoned-on" look** without making buttonholes by sewing flat buttons over Velcro or snap closures. I don't recommend shank buttons for this, as they can flop over and look untidy.

❖ **Explore pinning possibilities.** Button safety pins are sold wherever you find sewing notions. They are made with a "hump" to accommodate the button. You can use these pins to attach nonwashable buttons to washable garments or other projects. They are also a good solution for a quick repair, but be careful that the pin does not distort or damage delicate fabrics.

❖ **Grab the glue.** I use E-6000 glue very liberally for the projects in this book. Not only does it provide a secure bond, but it can be machine washed and dried (but *not* dry cleaned) without drying out or cracking, and it will not damage your buttons.

Threading buttons together with copper beading wire is easy to do and adds some flash to this bracelet. Instructions for this project begin on page 50.

❖ **Try wire and rings.** Beading or jewelry wire, as well as earring findings and hooks, make it easy to combine buttons for bracelets, necklaces and earrings when you'd rather not use thread. Split rings and jump rings let you easily attach shank buttons to a variety of projects.

❖ **Make a loop.** Don't forget to consider a loop closure if it can do the job. For a good example of this, see the necklace closure on page 44.

Shanks on plastic buttons can be removed easily and cleanly using diagonal or flush cutters. The shanks on most other buttons cannot be removed successfully without a grinding wheel or similar tool. However, I do *not* recommend destroying your buttons by removing their shanks. There are many ways you can attach buttons to projects without damaging them.

HANGING BY A THREAD

Most people will tell you to double your sewing thread on your needle to make the job of sewing on a button go faster, but I always seem to spend more time attempting to keep the threads even with every pull of the needle! My solution? Use a single thread that's stronger to begin with. Topstitching or jeans-stitching thread will speed up the process without the tangled mess that occurs when you work with a double thread. Polyester thread is stronger than cotton thread, but I still prefer perle cotton for sewing or tying buttons onto a project. It's strong *and* pretty!

Note: *Always choose thread that makes sense for the project. For example, you wouldn't want to use a heavy perle cotton thread to attach a button to a lightweight silk blouse.*

things to wear

Bring personality to shirts, necklaces, hats, handbags
and more by bringing on the buttons.

Here Comes the Sunflower Vest

This project is very versatile—choose a vest, jacket, skirt, bag or any other ready-made item to embellish.
A quilting stencil in the form of a simple feather circle design is used for the sunflower pattern. Using a stencil
will allow you to increase or decrease the pattern size to fit the area you wish to decorate. Look through your quilting
stencils and patterns and I bet you'll find more great ways to use them to help revive a garment in need of new life!

WHAT YOU'LL NEED

Assorted buttons:
at least 20

Vest

Felted wool:
1 fat quarter in gold and 1 fat quarter in brown

Fusible interfacing:
single-sided, lightweight*

Perle cotton

Stencil
*(a 9½" [24cm] feather circle design
was used for this project)*

Tracing pencil

Seam sealant

Large-eye needle

**Lightweight will be easier to hand-stitch through
and softer on the garment, but make sure
it's substantial enough to support
the weight of the buttons.*

Make a matching pin to dress up the collar. This would also make a great accent on a hat, purse or greeting card.

Sunflower Pin

1. Trace the larger of the patterns provided onto the brown wool and cut it out.

2. Trace the smaller pattern on the leftover scrap of gold felted wool. Cut it out, center it over the larger brown piece and glue it down. (I fused the small piece to the large piece using a scrap of fusible web. You can use fabric glue or E-6000 if you prefer.)

3. Stack 2 or more buttons in the center of the flower, and sew through all layers with the perle cotton. Finish with a square knot on the top of each button. Seal the knot with seam sealant.

4. Use E-6000 glue to attach a pin back. If desired, you can add a scrap strip of wool across the pin back with the E-6000, to hold it more securely.

Vest Back

1. Trace the stencil center circle onto the brown wool and the interfacing. Cut out the circle shape on the line on the wool piece, and about ¼" (6mm) inside the line on the interfacing so that it doesn't stick out from under the wool. The interfacing will give the wool a bit more stability while you stitch. Fuse it to the wrong side of the wool piece.

2. Trace the outline of the stencil flower petals onto the gold wool and the interfacing. Cut out as you did for the center piece and fuse the interfacing to the wrong side of the wool piece.

3. Sew the buttons onto the center circle using the perle cotton. I chose to tie a square knot on the top of each button to attach it. Use a drop of seam sealant on each knot to keep it from coming undone. **Note:** Besides a variety of color options (all black, all brown or a mix), there are many great options for arranging the buttons. Vary their sizes (as I did) or the spacing between them, or build a base layer of buttons and then stack and stagger them 2 and 3 high for dimension.

4. Sew the center piece onto the flower shape with perle cotton. Sew the whole piece onto your garment, again with the perle cotton. I used a stem stitch to define the petals first, then a blanket stitch around the outside.

WHAT YOU'LL NEED

Buttons:
2 or more, large, stackable

Sunflower pin patterns
(page 122)

Felted wool:
*1 scrap of dark brown;
1 scrap of gold (left over from vest project)*

Fusible web scrap

Perle cotton

Pin back

Tracing pencil

E-6000 glue

Seam sealant

Large-eye needle

Dressed-Up Denim Shirt

Coupling decorative buttons with an embroidered design is an easy way to breathe new life into an old or simply lackluster garment. Consider using stencils to add that touch of style and make a project that's designer made—by you! Stencils are available at quilt shops and craft and art supply stores. Use all of a pattern, a portion, or combine parts of two stencils. Make them any size you want by shrinking or enlarging them on a photocopier. Lay your buttons on the stencil to audition your favorites and plan their placement. Use a little, or a lot—it's up to you.

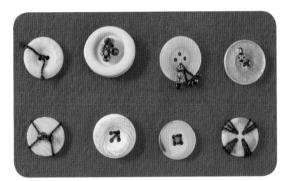

Experiment with different ways of sewing on buttons and incorporating small beads that will add a little more texture and interest.

1 Transfer the stencil design onto your shirt using a chalk pencil.

2 Embroider the design, using perle cotton and a large-eye needle. I chose a stem stitch for this design due to its many curves, for a smoother outline. **Note:** If you want to use yarn or ribbon, you can *couch* it on by machine (a method of stitching down one thread with another), or skip the sewing and iron it on using double-sided fusible tape.

3 Use basting glue to attach the buttons before stitching them on. This way you can sew them on with a single long running stitch, if desired—and you don't have to keep setting your project down to add a new button. Run your needle under previous stitching between buttons to avoid catching threads when you wear your garment. Create more flair by adding small beads as you sew on your buttons, using your beading needle.

RECYCLED, WITH LOVE

When my oldest son, Chad, went to college, he left a lot of things behind. Many moms can empathize with the experience of having a child leave home—as well as with the experience of wondering what to do with all their stuff. I found a way to make my son's denim work jacket wearable for me by adding crocheted appliqués, lace and lots of pearl buttons in a variety of shapes and sizes to embellish the collar, back yoke and other areas. The trick to this project was to hold the buttons in place on the fabric with small pieces of wash-away basting tape (available in various widths) so that I could use a single running stitch to quickly attach them. This jacket reminds me of my son every time I wear it!

"Hold It Right There!" Apron

Have you ever wished you could have all your sewing tools at your fingertips? This crafty apron will keep everything right where you need it, while keeping stray threads off of your clothes. Besides, it's just too darn cute!

Choosing an Apron Pattern

I chose the Indygo Junction pattern (view 1) for three reasons:

✿ The pattern showcases fun fabrics well and has large areas for "buttonability." Plus, the directions are simple and clear.

✿ The back covers only below the waist. I have tried to sit, then stand, then sit wearing a full-coverage apron and I find myself constantly tugging and adjusting the apron so that it doesn't choke me. The half-back pattern eliminates this.

✿ I love the pockets on this apron, as they create even more storage space. Just be sure to cover sharp points on tools such as scissors or metal rulers, as these might poke through the fabric and damage your apron (or you!) when you sit down.

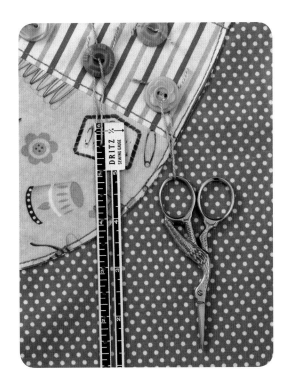

WHAT YOU'LL NEED

Assorted buttons

Apron pattern
*(Indygo Junction's "Stylish Smock" [IJ731]
was used for this project;
see Resources, page 126)*

Fabrics in coordinating colors and prints
(see pattern for amounts)

Felt:
1 small scrap

Perle cotton

Coordinating thread

Pinking shears

Basic sewing supplies
(including machine)

Design Details

✿ When choosing buttons, consider how often you'll need to wash your apron (see pages 18-19 for tips on picking buttons). The number of buttons is up to you. My preference for this project is "more is more." This is for you to wear in your private sewing sanctuary, so have fun and forget the fashion police!

✿ Cut a scrap of felt approximately 3" × 5" (8cm × 13cm). Pink the edges and cut a slit 1" (25mm) down from the top. Make this slit just large enough to slip the felt over a button. Now you have a place to keep your threaded needle and spare pins. Be sure to remove it if you wash the apron.

✿ Use perle cotton to tie loops through your small scissors, ruler, even a spare bobbin or spool for thread. No excuses for not sewing on that lost button now!

Your buttons don't have to stay indoors! Add them to a hat and you can show them off wherever you go.

Make several bands and you can change them to match your mood and your outfit.

1 If you are using ⅝" (16mm) ribbon, you may want to join 2 lengths of ribbon to make a wider band, as I did. Measure the circumference of your hat band area and add 10" (25cm). Cut 2 lengths of ribbon to this measurement. Butt the 2 pieces together and join them using a small zigzag or decorative stitch on your sewing machine. This now forms the band.

2 Place the ribbon around the hat, overlapping the ends at the back. Pin and stitch in place.

3 Cut 3 pieces of ribbon 14" (36cm) long and tie a bow from each piece. Place the bows, one above the other, at the back of the band. You can stitch them on by hand, or glue them on with E-6000.

4 Lay out your buttons in a pleasing arrangement and sew or glue them onto your band. You can cover the ribbon completely, or add a small nosegay of buttons. The choice is yours!
Note: This project may not be the best place to use buttons with large shanks, which will flop around rather than lie flat. If you choose to use a shank button, try placing a small scrap of batting behind the ribbon when you sew it on, to add stability. Once you try on the hat, the ribbon will be pulled taut and the button should stay flat.

WHAT YOU'LL NEED

Assorted buttons
(about 18 were used for this project)

Hat with brim

Ribbon:
3 yards (275cm) (⅝" wide was used for this project)

E-6000 glue

Coordinating thread

Basic sewing supplies
(machine optional)

Button-Adorned Mini Purses

The zippered mini would make a fine coin purse, cosmetics carrier or jewelry bag. Buttons needn't be the same color, but they should be the same size to achieve the desired effect. The style of the individual button isn't as important as the effect created when they're grouped together. Often, in a button box, you will find buttons that match on a safety pin or sewn on a thread, so start digging. They would be perfect for this purse! All those plain black and white shirt buttons could even make an elegant evening bag— just top them with a shiny bead and put them on fancy fabric.

The other envelope-style mini, with a Velcro closure, is a cute and compact way to carry business cards or any small item. It's a great gift card holder, especially when personalized for the recipient or occasion. This one is embellished with a single beautiful button, but use as many buttons as you like.

Zippered Mini Purse

Prepare the Purse Layers

1 Trace the pattern provided and transfer all markings onto tracing paper with a pen.

2 Cut 2 of the pattern from each: the purse fabric, lining fabric and batting. Trim off the upper edge seam allowance from the batting layers, as indicated on the pattern.

3 Layer a batting piece over the wrong side of a purse piece, matching outer edges and notches. Baste the 2 pieces together along the outside edge at ¼" (6mm). Pin on a lining piece, wrong side to the batting. This is the bag front.

4 For the bag back, repeat, but layer all 3 pieces together at once and baste together around the outside edge.

Shorten and Attach the Zipper

1 Close the zipper and measure from the tab top, along the zipper, and place a mark at 5⅛" (13cm) (see figure 1).

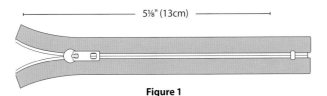

Figure 1

2 Using heavy-duty thread, make several overcast stitches, by hand, across the zipper teeth at the mark. Cut away the lower end of the zipper about ½" (13mm) from the overcast stitches (see figure 2).

3 Press under ½" (13mm) on the upper edges of the front and back bag pieces, treating both layers as 1 piece.

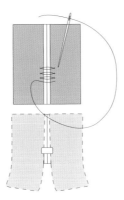

Figure 2

4 Pin the closed zipper, face up, under the opening edges of the bag sections, with the ends at the large dots (indicated on the pattern) and the opening edges meeting at the center of the zipper. Baste in place. Using a zipper foot on your machine, topstitch ¼" (6mm) on each side of the center (see figure 3).

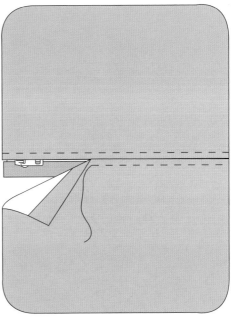

Figure 3

continue until
thread grid is
complete

—————— = on top of fabric
------------ = under fabric and batting

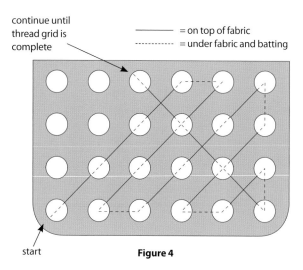

start

Figure 4

Embellish and Finish

1 Remove the pins from the front piece of the purse. Fold the lining piece toward the back piece and pin so that it is out of your way.

2 Working through both the top and batting layers, attach your buttons. (The knots will be covered by the lining piece when you are done.) To make the thread grid, come up under (but not through) a button on the outer edge of the grid and run the needle under each button in a diagonal line. At the end button, go through to the back and come up under the next row of buttons (see figure 4). Continue making the grid until it is complete. Remove the pins and replace the lining piece.

3 Open the zipper. With the purse fabric right sides together, stitch the front and back bag sections together (all 6 layers) along the outer edges, matching the notches. Use a ½" (13mm) seam allowance. Serge or zigzag-stitch the seam allowances.

4 Turn the bag to the outside through the zipper opening. Press if needed.

5 Attach a split ring to the hole in the zipper tab and add a button to the ring for a stylish and easy way to pull the zipper open and closed.

Envelope-Style Mini Purse

1 Cut the felt into a rectangle that measures 7" x 4½" (18cm x 11cm).

2 Sew the ribbon on down the center of the felt using a small zigzag stitch, folding the raw edges under at both ends.

3 Lay the rectangle on a table in front of you with the short sides at top and bottom, ribbon side down. Measure 2½" (6cm) up from the bottom of the rectangle on both sides and mark with a pin.

4 Fold the end nearest you at these marks. Stitch on each side to create the envelope.

5 Place Velcro pieces on the inside flap and corresponding spot on the envelope. **Note:** I like to use a dab of E-6000 glue for added adhesion. Let it dry thoroughly. Placing your envelope under a heavy book or the like will ensure that you get a good bond that will stand up to frequent use.

6 Add an eye-catching button to the front, either by sewing it on or by gluing it on with adhesive. Add multiple buttons if you'd like.

WHAT YOU'LL NEED

Buttons:
1 or more

Felt

Ribbon

Coordinating thread

Velcro closure

E-6000 glue

Basic sewing supplies
(including machine)

Weave-and-Leave Mini Tote

This versatile little tote was inspired by a great button find and some purchased wool scraps. I wanted a sturdy little bag to carry a book, some handwork or a snack for a day trip. The buttons on this project have a channel-style shank so they lie flat on the bag front. If you choose a regular shank button that needs support to keep it from flopping over, consider using a felt "penny" disk: cut a small slit in the disk, pass the shank through the slit and sew the button on. The felt acts like a washer for a screw or bolt, keeping your button in place. This bag would also look great made with a leftover quilt block for the front—accented by great buttons, of course!

Bag Body

1 From the red wool, cut 2 rectangles that measure 11½" x 8¾" (29cm x 22cm). Set one aside for the bag back.

2 On the front of the second piece, measure 2" (5cm) up from the bottom on the longer sides and mark with a pin. Next, measure 1" (25mm) down from the top on the longer sides and mark with a pin.

3 From the wool for the woven strips, cut 8 strips that measure 1" x 8½" (25mm x 22cm).

4 Start with the horizontal strips. Place the first strip at the top (1" [25mm]) pin, and the last strip at the bottom (2" [5cm]) pin. Leave a 1" (25mm) space between each of the 5 strips.

5 Next, weave the 3 vertical strips into the horizontal strips, centering the middle strip and leaving a 1" (25mm) space between the other 2 strips.

6 Use tiny dots of tacky glue to baste the strips in place. Trim the horizontal strips at the edges of the red fabric. Trim the 3 vertical strips so that they do not extend beyond the pin marks.

7 Topstitch the strips in place.

8 With right sides together, and using a ½" (13mm) seam, stitch the red wool pieces together on 3 sides, leaving the top open.

9 Press the seams open. To make the bag bottom, pinch the side seam and bottom seam so that they line up on top of each other. Measure 1½" (38mm) up from the point and stitch a line across to form a triangle (see figure 1). Do the same on the other side of the bag.

10 Add the buttons by stitching them to the front of the bag in a grid. (Follow the photo on page 35 for suggested placement.)

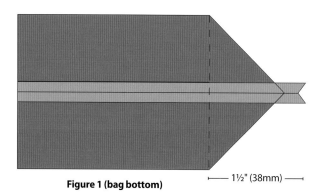

Figure 1 (bag bottom)

├─── 1½" (38mm) ───┤

Lining and Finishing

Make the lining in the same way as the bag.

1. From the lining fabric, cut 2 rectangles that measure 11½" x 8¾" (29cm x 22cm).

2. Place the right sides together and stitch up 3 sides using a scant ½" (13mm) seam, so the lining will fit inside the bag body with some ease.

3. Make the bottom corners in the same way as described in step 9 on page 36. Turn the red wool bag body right side out. Do not turn the lining; insert it into the bag body so that the wrong sides of each bag are touching. Line up the seams and square up the bottoms.

4. Fold the inner lining at the 1" (25mm) pin line. Fold the red wool over the top of the lining at the 1" (25mm) pin line.

5. Topstitch the lining and wool bag together around the bag top.

6. Cut the belt webbing in half (in this example, each piece is 18" [46cm]). Center and topstitch a piece of wool (left over from the strips cut for the bag front) that is slightly narrower in width on top of the webbing (see photo).

7. Attach the straps to the inside of the bag by stitching over the previous topstitching.

It's in the Handbag

The size of this bag— 9¼" × 5¼" (24cm × 13cm)—makes it perfect for carrying your essentials and keeping them close to you, especially while shopping. I've found this size also works well for toting my button-collecting tools at flea markets. Increase the size to hold a book, or decrease it to hold a tube of lipstick and ID for a night on the town. Add pockets to the inside lining to make finding small things easier. No matter the size of your bag, one thing is for sure: your favorite buttons will look stunning on it!

The back of the bag.

1 Using the pattern provided, cut 2 from the bag fabric and 2 from the lining fabric.

2 Embellish the front piece of the bag as desired. I used a leftover scrap of lace under the photo transfer. The lace was machine stitched around the outside edge using matching thread. The photo is embellished with a feather stitch and beads. Other embellishments used include buttons, beads, embroidery stitches and silk ribbon flowers.

3 With right sides together, sew the bag front and back together using a ¼" (6mm) seam allowance. Remember to leave the top open. Turn the bag right side out.

4 Sew the lining pieces together in the same manner, but do not turn the lining right side out once you're finished. Set this aside.

5 Cut the strap cord to the desired length, plus about 4" (10cm). Satin stitch over the ends of the cord and apply seam sealant so the cord does not unravel. Fold up each end of the cord about 1" (25mm) and place these on the inside of the bag at the side seams.

6 Place a large sew-through button on the outside of the bag at the top on each side. Sew through each button and cord end with a heavy thread such as perle cotton to hold the strap in place.

7 Insert the lining into the bag, matching the side seams and covering the cord on the inside. Turn the top of both the bag and the lining down ½" (13mm) to the inside. Topstitch closed.

Well-Dressed Wristlet Purses

Who says you have to make every project from scratch? There are many blank canvasses out there begging
to be embellished. My favorite places to hunt for treasures to decorate include craft stores, yard sales,
flea markets and thrift stores—even my sister-in-law's closet. Everything is fair game for a makeover.
Once you start working with your buttons in this way, opportunities for creativity will suddenly appear.
Just keep asking yourself, "Where can I put a button on that?" These little purses are a great example.
Round up your trims and buttons to "purse-onalize" an otherwise plain surface!

Technique Tips

Your imagination is the key to this project, so a few pointers on technique are all you'll need.

❈ It's best to leave your buttons in their original state, so don't cut off their shanks if you can avoid it. One of the best ways to attach shank buttons is to anchor them to a trim piece before attaching them to your project. Sew (preferable) or glue (with E-6000) your buttons to a trim or ribbon. If the trim has holes in it (such as the flowers in the photo), set the shank inside a hole. The trim will hold the button level, while the shank will be hidden. Use a dab of E-6000 on the underside of the button to hold it in place.

❈ Ribbon or cord can be threaded through a button shank and then woven into an opening such as the one at the top of these purses.

❈ Yo-yos, ribbon flowers and stacked wool "pennies" can be great settings for your buttons, like gemstones in a ring.

❈ When choosing buttons for a project, don't overlook the plain Janes. Use them at the bottom of a stack of buttons to give size, color and texture to your project. Start with the largest, flat button and build up to the smallest button. If that top

WHAT YOU'LL NEED

Assorted buttons*

Purse

Assorted trims*

E-6000 glue

Seam sealant

Decorative thread or yarn
(optional)

Basic sewing supplies
(optional)

*Because you probably won't need to wash your purse, you can choose any buttons or trims you wish!

button is a shank button, you can sew it to the button below it and once again avoid cutting the shank off. Use fun, colorful thread or yarn to sew the stack together on the "outside" of the buttons (see page 27), and you've got a work of art!

❈ Another benefit to using trims is that you can then glue your embellishments to your project without piercing the lining of your purse. I still prefer to use a needle and thread to attach embellishments when possible, but a dab of adhesive is a good backup. Always use seam sealant on any knots you tie.

Knot-Your-Ordinary Necklace

I have long admired crocheted button necklaces, but try as they did, my grandmothers could not teach me to crochet!
This necklace is my solution. It enables me to mix buttons and beads in a very simply constructed necklace.
The possible combinations are endless!

Design Details

✿ A basic necklace has three strand sets, but you can use as many as you like. Three sets will fit into the crimp tube. If you use more strands or a thicker thread, you can use a different type of necklace closure, or perhaps form a macramé-style loop with the extra thread on the end and team it with a button to complete the closure (see page 44).

✿ If you choose to string beads with your buttons, use beads with holes large enough to accommodate each two-thread strand set. I selected complementary bead sizes, using several large beads in the style that I liked best, interspersed with groups of smaller beads whose total width equals (or almost equals) that of each large bead. For example, if the large bead is 1" (25mm), complement it with a pair of ½" (13mm) beads, or a group of three 3mm beads.

✿ The number and size of the buttons you use is up to you. When stringing all three strand sets together at the same lengths, I like to use five buttons and six beads (or bead groups) in one set, then six buttons and five beads (or bead groups) in the other sets. However, for the necklace shown—with strand sets of varying lengths—I used seven buttons and six bead groups in one set, six buttons and five bead groups in the second set, and four buttons with five beads in the third set.

WHAT YOU'LL NEED

Buttons:
7 large red, 6 medium-sized black,
4 medium-sized red and 1 large red for optional button-and-loop closure, all sew-through style

Crochet thread:
nylon, size 2, 6 yards (548cm)

Beads:
15 red, ¼" (6mm); 12 black, ⅜" (10mm);
5 red/black/white, ½" (13mm)

3 jump rings

Crimp tubes:
2 with a ⅛" (3mm) opening

Lobster claw clasp

Chain for the extension
3" (8cm) (optional)

Straight pin

Beading needle with collapsible eye

Needle-nose pliers

Basic Construction

Cut the thread into 6 pieces measuring 1 yard (91cm) each; 2 threads equal 1 strand set.

For Each Strand Set

1 Find the center of the threads and weave them over or under the first button, through the holes. Make sure the button is centered and then tie an overhand knot, using both threads as one, on either side of the button to hold it in place. Use the straight pin to help guide the knot in place. When it is in position, pull out the pin and pull the knot tight. **Note:** Your center button might in fact be a bead. In that case, you'll begin by centering the bead and tying an overhand knot on either side to hold it in place.

2 Measure 1" (25mm) from one of the knots and tie another knot. Do the same on the other side of the center button. Add a bead (or bead group) on each side, stringing both threads through the bead hole. If you cannot string both threads through the hole easily, use the beading needle to help pull them through. Tie a knot to hold the beads in place.

3 Continue in this manner, with a knot on either side of a button or bead (or bead group), leaving 1" (25mm) between them, until all buttons and beads are on the strand set.

To Finish the Necklace

1 When all 3 strand sets are completed, thread the 6 thread ends through a crimp tube. You will find the first few easy to thread; use the beading needle to pull the rest through. Do the same to the other side, being careful not to unthread the first side.

2 Lay the necklace on a table, positioning the threads to lie correctly. Ensure that the crimp tubes are equidistant on either side. Use the pliers to press the tube closed to lock the threads in place. Tug on the threads to make sure they are secure.

3 Add a jump ring to the end of each crimp tube, and the lobster claw to one of the rings.

4 If you wish, add a length of chain to the jump ring that does not have the clasp. For a fun finish, add a jump ring and button to the opposite end of the chain (see both styles of closures—with and without the optional extender—on page 45).

If you wish, you can add a macramé-style loop-and-button closure. Knot the threads together and seal with seam sealant. Use a single thread to (single) chain over the other threads (tie a slipknot, reach through the loop with your fingers, grab the thread tail and pull through; repeat). Knot again and seal. Tie a loop in place. Attach the button by threading through it, knotting on the underside and sealing.

For matching earrings, buy hoop earring findings at your local craft store and simply thread small buttons with a bead between them onto the loop. Bend the end over and try them on!

Bead-free button necklaces can be just as stunning. The foreground necklace combines buttons in an array of beautiful autumn colors. The necklace in the background showcases coconut buttons in rich earth tones.

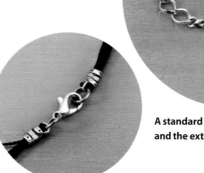

A standard lobster-claw clasp closure, and the extender chain option.

Two-Faced (in a Nice Way) Necklace

This reversible necklace can be made with buttons of any size, as long as the ones you choose are uniform in size and have the same number of holes. Make yours from an odd collection of buttons, or from matching groups, such as this one. Embellishing beads can be multicolored, or match the buttons. The necklace can be made in any length; this one is 24" (61cm). Simply cut your stretchy cord approximately one and a half times the length of the desired necklace.

Contributed by Jay Staten

1 Thread 1 end of the cord through 1 crimp connector. Use crimping pliers to crimp securely.

2 Thread the opposite end of the cord through the back of a deep teal button. Then thread on 1 blue seed bead.

3 Thread the cord through the opposite hole on the front of the button. The seed bead should sit between the 2 holes on the front of the button.

4 Thread the cord through the back of an aqua/green button. Then thread on 1 green seed bead.

WHAT YOU'LL NEED

Buttons:
flat, 4-hole, sew-through style, ½" (13mm);
(46 deep teal and 45 aqua/green buttons
were used for this project)

Elastic jewelry cord:
0.7 mm, clear, 1 yard (91cm)

Seed beads
(46 blue and 45 green were used for this project)

Necklace clasp
(a screw-on barrel clasp was used for this project)

2 crimp connectors

Crimping pliers

Scissors

5 Thread the cord through the opposite hole on the front of the button.

6 Repeat steps 2-5, 45 times. **Note:** Keep the stretchy cord even, but do not pull it taut. This will give your necklace flexibility.

7 Thread the end of the cord through the second crimp connector. Use crimping pliers to crimp securely. Cut off any excess cord.

8 Attach a necklace clasp.

Button-Lover Bangles

I love to wear bracelets; my jewelry box is full of them! Some of the bangle bracelets in my collection were looking outdated, so I gave them a makeover by pairing a ribbon-wrapping technique with the addition of buttons.

Multicolored Bracelet

1 Apply a dab of E-6000 glue with the toothpick to the inside of the bracelet. Lay the end of the ribbon over the adhesive, press firmly, and allow it to dry for about 10 minutes.

2 Start to wrap the ribbon around the bracelet, pulling tightly and overlapping each layer slightly. Cover the bracelet completely, ending on the inside and anchoring the ribbon end with another dab of E-6000.

3 Thread the length of perle cotton onto the needle. Make a small knot in the end of the floss. Take a small stitch in the ribbon on the inside of the bracelet. Bring the floss to the front of the bracelet and thread 2 larger buttons onto the floss. Wrap the floss to the back at a slight angle and bring it to the front again. Thread 3 smaller buttons onto the floss. Place this row of buttons close to the first row.

Repeat this process of wrapping and threading on buttons of various sizes. Once in a while, take a stitch through the ribbon on the inside of the bracelet to anchor the buttons in place. End with another anchor stitch and knot on the inside.

4 Cut a strip of felt whose width measures just short of the width of the inside of the bracelet (if you make it too wide it will show to the front). Lay it inside the bracelet and cut the length so that the ends "kiss." Glue it in place with tacky glue.

MIX IT UP

Now that you have a base to work from, why not add some beads to the tops of the sew-through buttons? Add shank buttons by placing them in between sew-through button rows, which will support the shank buttons while hiding their shanks.

WHAT YOU'LL NEED

Assorted buttons:
various sizes and colors

Plastic bangle bracelet

Felt for lining the bracelet

Ribbon:
¼" (6mm) wide, 2-3 yards (2-3m)

Perle cotton:
1 yard (91cm), in a coordinating or contrasting color

E-6000 glue

Tacky glue

Tapestry needle
(sharp point, large eye)

Scissors

Toothpick

This bracelet uses ⅛" (3mm) black ribbon. The buttons have had their shanks removed and were affixed to the ribbon using E-6000 glue. Normally I wouldn't remove shanks, but I made a rare exception with these, an inexpensive store purchase.

Two Tones, One Bracelet

Copper wire and colorful buttons make a wonderful combination! This 7" (18cm) bracelet can be made with a multitude of buttons, but size is important. When using buttons more than ½" (13mm) in diameter, the bracelet will not bend to conform to your wrist. Consider adding a large attention-getter to the center for special interest.

Contributed by Jay Staten

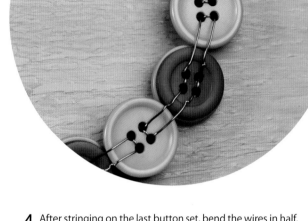

1 Arrange your buttons in the desired order. Here, blue and green buttons alternate, back to back.

2 Cut 2 strands of wire approximately 20" (51cm) long. Tape 1 end of the wires together to temporarily secure.

3 Thread each wire through side-by-side holes on the front of the first green button. Guide each wire through the back of the blue button directly below it, then thread each wire down through the hole directly across. Continue adding button sets in this manner. This means that you will have 2 strands of wire moving side by side down the length of the buttons (see photo). **Hint:** To secure the buttons back to back, consider using a spot of glue to hold them together.

4 After stringing on the last button set, bend the wires in half.

5 Thread the folded ends of wire through the crimp connector. Use crimping pliers to crimp securely.

6 Thread the wire back through the buttons, starting on the opposite side. After reaching the end, cut off the excess wire.

7 Thread all 4 wire ends through a crimp connector. Use crimping pliers to crimp securely. Add a clasp.

WHAT YOU'LL NEED

Buttons:
flat, 4-hole, sew-through style, ½" (13mm);
(12 green and 12 blue were used for this project)

Beading wire:
18-gauge copper, 60" (152cm)

Crimp connectors

Clasp

Tape

E-6000 glue
(optional)

Wire cutters

Dazzling Dangle Earrings

The possibilities are endless when combining buttons and beads to create earrings.

Don't be afraid to dexperiment—earrings do not have to be perfectly identical to be attractive.

Contributed by Jay Staten

Short Pair

1 Cut a 3" (8cm) length of wire, then fold it in half. String the wire through the bottom loop of the ear hook.

2 String both ends of the wire through 1 roble wood bead, then separate the wires.

3 Add 2 buttons back to back by stringing 1 wire through the back top hole of 1 button, and the other wire through the back top hole of the other button.

4 On the front of each button, string wire through 1 round bead.

5 String each wire through the bottom hole of each button, from front to back.

6 Twist the wires together, pulling the buttons tight. Cut off the excess wire. Repeat all steps for the second earring.

Long Pair

1 Cut a 3" (8cm) length of wire. Secure the wire to the bottom loop of the ear hook.

2 String the wire through 1 roble wood bead.

3 String the wire through the back top hole of button 1.

4 On the front of button 1, string the wire through 1 round bead.

5 String the wire through the bottom hole of button 1 and into the back top hole of button 2.

6 On front of button 2, string the wire through 1 round bead.

7 String the wire through the bottom hole of button 2 and into back top hole of button 3.

8 On the front of button 3, string the wire through 1 round bead.

9 String the wire through the bottom hole of button 3, then string the wire through 1 round bead on the back of that button.

10 Secure the end of the wire around the back of button 2, hidden behind buttons 1 and 3. Cut off the excess wire. Repeat all steps for the second earring.

Bloomin' Brooches

Freshen up the look of a coat, blazer or purse by adding a button-flower brooch. Rotate a variety
of pins according to the season or occasion. The first brooch's soft, pink petals direct attention to the fine detail
of the beautiful center button; the all-button approach of the second brooch emphasizes its fun colors and shape.

Single-Button Brooch

1 Choose a button that is similar in size to the silk flower center. Glue the button to the flat tie-tack surface with E-6000 glue, creating a button pin. If you're using a shank button (as pictured), choose wisely (nothing expensive or valuable) and remove the shank using diagonal cutters.

2 Remove the plastic center from the silk flower and replace it with the button pin. Change the flower with the seasons for a very versatile accent!

WHAT YOU'LL NEED

Button

Tie tack finding

Silk flower

E-6000 glue

Diagonal cutters
(optional)

WHAT YOU'LL NEED

Buttons:
5-6 matching sew-through style, medium size; 1 sew-through style, large size, in a complementary color; 1 sew-though style, small size, in a complementary color

Pin back

E-6000 glue

All-Button Brooch

Contributed by Rachael Smith

1 With your 5 or 6 matching buttons, make a ring. Place a small dab of E-6000 glue on the bottom center of each button. Place the large button, making sure it is centered, on top of the smaller buttons and press. Place a small dab of glue onto the center of the large button and press the small button on top of that.

2 Turn over the glued button piece. Eyeball the size of your pin back, then place a small dab of glue onto the left and right sides toward the middle of your button piece, or a little closer to the top. Press the pin back in place.

Gluing Tips

✿ Be sure to use only E-6000 glue, because the chemical makeup of the adhesive is such that it will not damage your buttons.

✿ Glue the flat surface of the small button to the flat surface of the large button. You could glue the raised sides together, but they may not hold as well.

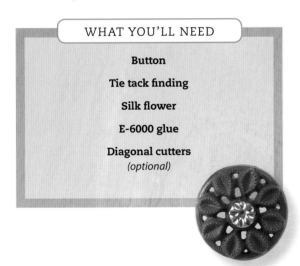

for your home

Show off a single spectacular button

or incorporate many into a quilt, picture frame or pillow.

Button-Beautified Frames

Buttons can have a huge impact when grouped together on your projects. Even your plainest and most common buttons can make a textural statement. For this project, use non-valuable buttons that can be cut and glued.

General Tips

✿ The hardest part of this project is being happy with your arrangement. I've found I spend too much time arranging and rearranging my buttons, and what I've learned is that my first grouping was the best after all. There is no right or wrong. Trust your instincts and just "glue" it!

✿ Normally, the last thing I want to do is encourage anyone to cut the shanks off their buttons. For this project, however, it may be necessary, so be selective with the buttons you choose. If you'd like to use a shank button and removing the shank is not advised or possible, use other buttons or trims to create a "nest" in which to set the shank. The wonderful thing about using E-6000 glue is that it takes such a small amount to securely hold your buttons, and it won't damage them, either.

✿ Experiment with button color, size and dimension in this project. Combine your buttons with trims and other decorative items. My only word of caution would be to remember that your photo is the center of attention, and the button composition should never overpower your subject.

WHAT YOU'LL NEED

Assorted buttons

Picture frame:
fabric or wood, any size

Assorted trims
(optional)

E-6000 glue

Diagonal cutters
(optional)

"I Was Framed!" Buttons

Buttons are truly miniature works of art, so why not treat them as such? Frame them and you have an instant gallery piece. This is a great way to display your special buttons. The recommended adhesive will not harm them so they can easily be removed if you choose to do so later. Try lots of different frame and fabric styles with your buttons. You'll be amazed how beautiful they are in any setting!

1 Remove the backing piece from the frame and trace around it on the foamcore board.

2 Cut out the shape from the foamcore board with the craft knife. Make sure it fits snugly into the frame.

3 Using the craft knife, cut a hole in the foamcore board for each button shank to nest in so it will sit flat on the board. **Hint:** Start small! If your button has a large metal shank, you may choose to have the hole go completely through the foamcore board. If your button has an integrated (or self) shank, as do many glass and vegetable ivory buttons, your hole should be shallow, but wide.

Note: If your fabric has a pattern that you want to follow when placing your buttons, then:

- Lay your fabric in place on the foamcore board.

- Use a pin to poke a small hole through the fabric to the foamcore to mark the placement for your holes.

- Remove the fabric and start to carve out the holes. If placement is critical or tricky, glue the fabric in place before finishing the holes (see step 4).

4 Cover the top of the foamcore board with spray adhesive. Place the fabric on top and smooth out any wrinkles. Locate the hole you made in the foamcore and, using the craft knife, cut a slit in the fabric for the button shank.

SEW INSTEAD OF GLUE

If you choose to use a sew-through button for your artwork, you can use a corn-cob holder to poke two small holes in your foamcore board and then sew the button on with a pretty perle cotton thread.

5 Place a tiny dab of E-6000 glue on the shank of your button and set it in place. If your hole goes through the foamcore board, you can guide a plastic-coated wire through the shank and wrap it flat against the back of the foamcore board.

6 Secure the "artwork" in the frame. This may be tricky; often the foamcore board is too thick to allow you to put the original back on the frame. If this is the case, apply small amounts of E-6000 glue on the inside rim of the frame and glue your piece into the frame. Cover the back of the frame with a piece of felt, using E-6000 to glue it to the outside of the frame.

Covered-Button Showcase Sampler

Grouped and arranged attractively, fabric-covered buttons make an interesting sampler. Give this project your own interpretation and flair. You can feature buttons covered with vintage fabrics, work with elegant velvet- and satin-covered buttons, or even round up buttons that show off leather and suede. Let the buttons you choose determine your background fabric. This small sampler measures 5½" × 7" (14cm × 18cm).

Contributed by Nancy Breen

1 Layer the backing fabric, batting and background fabric to make a "quilt sandwich." Use safety pins to secure the layers, starting in the middle and working outward.

2 Using a ruler and water-soluble fabric marker, draw 3 vertical lines dividing the sandwich into equal quarters (reposition the safety pins if they're in the way). Next, draw 3 horizontal lines to create equal quarters. Finally, draw diagonal lines through the center of the sandwich; diagonal lines should be proportional, but they don't have to meet the corners.

3 Lay out the buttons you'll be using on the background fabric, concentrating on line intersections and diagonal lines, and play with the arrangement until you get a pleasing design. Transfer the buttons to your work surface, arranging them in the same order.

4 Machine-quilt or hand-stitch along the vertical, horizontal and diagonal lines. Starting at the center, sew each button into place.

5 Trim the edges of the quilt just enough to even them up, but leave the edges raw. Center the quilt on the felt and secure it with safety pins. Machine- or hand-stitch the quilt to the felt ⅛" (3mm) from the raw edges.

6 Using pinking shears (or leave the edges straight if desired), trim the felt to within ¼" (6mm) on the sides and bottom. Fold the top 1" (25mm) in half and stitch along the edge to the back of the felt, creating a sleeve. Insert a small rod or narrow wooden dowel.

7 The sampler can be hung by positioning the ends of the rod or dowel over nails or push pins. If you prefer, use ribbon or cord for hanging instead, tying or sewing the ends of an 8" (20cm) piece to the rod or dowel.

WHAT YOU'LL NEED

Assorted buttons
(13 were used for this project)

Fabric for background:
5" x 6½" (13cm x 17cm)

Fabric for backing:
muslin or other type, 5" x 6½" (13cm x 17cm)

Felt:
wool or craft, 6" x 7½" (15cm x 19cm)

Batting:
5½" x 7½" (14cm x 19cm)

Narrow wooden rod or dowel:
at least 6" (15cm)

Ribbon or cord for hanging:
8" (20cm) (optional)

Coordinating thread

Water-soluble fabric marker

Small safety pins

Ruler

Pinking shears

Basic sewing supplies
(machine optional)

"Grandma's Button Box" Wall Hanging

Grandma's Button Box

My Grandma saved so many things
She thought that she might need
Like rubber bands and bits of foil
"Waste not" was her creed!
Now thanks to her I have this box
That's full as it can be
Of lovely little buttons
Such precious memories!
Just look at all these buttons!
Our family's history!
My Grandma saved them in this box
Oh lucky, lucky me!

So many button lovers who've inherited their grandmothers' buttons have shared with me their stories, recollections, discoveries and family memories related to these prized possessions. There is one thing they all have in common: everyone has a broad smile on their faces as they recount the special times they shared with Grandma and her buttons! I hope this 14¾" × 12¾" (38cm × 32cm) wall hanging, containing an abbreviated version of the poem on page 11, makes *you* smile.

Transfer the Poem

I will give very general directions for printing and transferring the poem to fabric. Please follow the manufacturer's instructions regarding properly preparing your fabric, as well as printing and transferring for best results.

1. Type the poem into a word-processing program on your computer. Choose a font style and size that you like. The poem needs to fit in a 5" x 7" (13cm x 18cm) rectangle. Your program's print preview feature is a great tool for checking your work before printing. *Be sure to select the mirror image option prior to printing.* Insert the transfer paper into your printer and print the poem.

2. Iron the white fabric to remove any wrinkles that may distort your image. This also aids in the transfer process. Place the image face down in the center of the fabric and transfer according to the manufacturer's instructions. Don't worry if it's not quite centered; you can trim it to the correct size later.

3. Once the piece is completely cool, center and trim the white fabric to 6" x 8" (15cm x 20cm). A transparent ruler will do this job best. **Hint:** If you line up the underline of the poem's title on the 1" (25mm) line (horizontally) and the 3" (8cm) line (vertically) between the "s" and the "B" in the title line, you should be centered.

Cut Your Fabric

1. With a pen or pencil, trace the pattern for the scalloped frame onto a piece of tracing paper. Pin the paper to the felt square and cut out the frame. You could also cut out the pattern first and transfer with a chalk pencil if you prefer.

2. From your print fabric, cut 2 pieces measuring 17" x 14" (43cm x 36cm).

WHAT YOU'LL NEED

Assorted buttons

Inner scalloped frame pattern
(page 124)

Fabric for center transfer:
white, 9" x 7" (23cm x 18cm)

**Fabric for borders,
back and hanging sleeve:**
print, ¾ yard (69cm)

Felt for inner frame:
contrasting color, 9" x 12" (23cm x 30cm)

Felted wool:
white or beige, 6" x 8" (15cm x 20cm)

Batting:
17" x 14" (43cm x 36cm)

Binding:
3 yards (274cm)

Coordinating thread

Perle cotton
(optional)

Basting glue
(optional)

Tracing paper

Transfer paper
(June Tailor Print 'n Press was used for this project)

Chalk pencil

Transparent ruler

Computer with word-processing software

Ink-jet printer

Basic sewing supplies
(including machine)

Assemble the Wall Hanging

1 Take a 17" x 14" (43cm x 36cm) piece of the print fabric and crease in both directions to find the center. Lay the piece right side up in front of you.

2 Find the center of the felted wool piece and lay it on top of the print fabric, matching the crease lines. Pin or baste using basting glue. Press the lines out of both pieces at this point. If you wait, you may accidentally iron the poem piece and ruin it.

3 Place your poem fabric on top of the felted wool piece and pin or baste.

4 Place the scalloped felt frame over the poem. I prefer using basting glue for this step so that the felt doesn't stretch or shift while sewing.

5 Take the assembled pieces to your machine and stitch all layers together ¼" (6mm) inside the frame lines.

6 Layer the second fabric piece (wrong side up), the batting piece and the poem piece (right side up), matching the edges. Pin. Using a long stitch length, baste the 3 layers together, by hand or machine, ¼" (6mm) in from the outside edges.

Add the Hanging Sleeve and Binding

1 Measure across the top of your quilt. Subtract 3" (8cm) from this measurement. Take this new number and cut a piece of print fabric that measures this length by 4½" (11cm) wide. For example, if your quilt measures 13" (33cm) across the top, your sleeve piece should measure 10" x 4½" (25cm x 11cm).

2 Fold under a narrow, double-turned seam on each 4½" (11cm) side. Press and stitch.

PICTURE THIS!

- Make a one-of-a-kind wedding gift by using the invitation and fancy white or ivory buttons on fabric that includes the bridal party colors.

- Hit one out of the park with sports fans by coupling a song such as "Take Me Out to the Ball Game" with novelty baseball buttons on fabric that shows off their favorite team's colors.

- Create a cherished keepsake for a new mom-to-be by pairing a nursery rhyme with baby-themed buttons on fabric that coordinates with the new little one's room.

- Give a graduation gift they'll never forget: a wall hanging that proudly displays their school's alma mater or fight song, along with buttons and fabric in the school's colors.

3 Center the sleeve on the back of the wall hanging, matching all raw edges at the top. Baste along the previous basting line.

4 Add the binding to the front of your quilt.

Finish Your Wall Hanging

1 Now is the best time to add your buttons. Use any type of thread you wish. I prefer perle cotton for its strength and color choices. You will also need fewer stitches, keeping the back of your piece neater. To keep your knots from showing on the back of your wall hanging, bury them behind the felt and then sew the buttons on through all layers. Knot behind the felt again to finish.

2 Finish the binding by folding it to the back and hand-stitching it in place. Now carefully hand-stitch the sleeve to the quilt back at the fold in the sleeve.

3 Insert a hanger through the sleeve and proudly display.

Grandma's Button Box

My Grandma saved so many things
She thought that she might need
Like rubber bands and bits of foil
"Waste not" was her creed!
Now thanks to her I have this box
That's full as it can be
Of lovely little buttons
Such precious memories!
These brass ones once were shiny
But not so anymore
They come from all the uniforms
Our family proudly wore!
Here's a shiny glass one
From her favorite dress of blue
And tiny pearls from my dress
That she made when I was two!
These white ones are just plain and round
From P_'s Grandpa wore
Until they got so paper thin
And the fabric finally tore!
My favorite one is yellow
Not really much to see
But it's from her robe she used to wear
When she would read to me!
Just look at all these buttons!
Our family's history!
My Grandma saved them in this box
Oh lucky, lucky me!

To embellish a mat as shown here, use an awl or ice pick to punch holes through the mat. Secure the buttons to the mat using plastic-coated wires (see page 14). Mount in a frame without glass, or in a shadow box where the glass will be a distance from the buttons.

Blooming Buttons Garden Quilt

Enjoy a lovely garden of flowers and memories on even the dreariest winter days with this cheery, adorable quilt.

Best of all, you never have to water it! With the creation of plastics in the 1920s, even buttons became subject to

mass production. The fun, colorful ones I used on this quilt were made in the 1930s and 40s.

This quilt, which measures 27½" × 22½" (70cm × 57cm), was expertly hand-quilted by Linda Schwarz
of Colorado Springs. She used two sizes of crosshatch in the center and echo stitching throughout.
Machine quilting would have required too much stopping and starting, due to the crosshatching involved.
Another option would be to quilt the piece before adding the flowers and buttons;
however, the knots where the buttons were sewn on would show on the back of the quilt.

Cutting Instructions

1. Trim the selvage from the white fabric, then cut a piece 15½" (39cm) by the width of the fabric. Cut this piece into 2 rectangles, 20½" x 15½" (52cm x 39cm) each. Set 1 piece aside for the center of the quilt. From the other, cut 2 strips 20½" x 3½" (52cm x 9cm) each and 2 strips 15½" x 3½" (39cm x 9cm) each.

2. From the green fabric, cut 2 strips 20½" x 1½" (52cm x 4cm) and 2 strips 15½" x 1½" (39cm x 4cm).

3. From the purple fabric, cut 1 strip 18" x 4½" (46cm x 11cm). Subcut this into 4 squares 4½" x 4½" (11cm x 11cm).

Construction

All seams are sewn with a scant ¼" (6mm) seam.

Form the Borders

1. Pair each green strip to a white strip of matching length and sew together lengthwise. Press the seam toward the green. Each pair should now measure 4½" (11cm) wide.

2. Refer to figure 1 on page 70. Lay a white/green strip on your work surface: white on top, green on bottom. Press a center crease across the width.

3. Measure 1¾" (4cm) from the top of the white strip and press a crease the length of the strip.

4. With the water-soluble marker, make the following marks in the white area of the border strip: ¼" (6mm) in from each side, ½" (13mm) down from the top, and ¼" (6mm) up from the seam.

5. Lay your ruler on the top marks and place a dot every 2½" (6cm) across the length of the strip. Do the same across the bottom of the strip.

6. Pin on the purple bias tape in a wave pattern, one side at a time, using the dots as guides. Leave a small tail on each end to be caught into the seam. The outer edge of the tape should touch the dots, and the tape should cross or peak at each 2½" (6cm) dot. Where the tapes cross, align the inner "V" with the center crease.

7. Remove the marks with a wet cotton swab and carefully press the bias tape flat.

8. Sew along both sides of the tape. Trim the tape even with the fabric edge in the seam allowance. Repeat steps 2-8 for the other strips.

Refer to figure 1 on page 70.

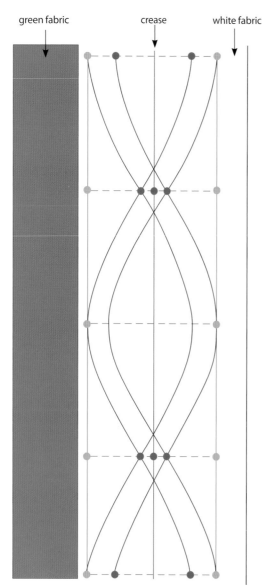

green fabric crease white fabric

Figure 1 (border)

Make the Center of the Quilt

1 Press a crease down the center and then across the middle of the 20½" x 15½" (52cm x 39cm) white center piece you set aside earlier.

2 Fold the sheet of paper in half widthwise and trace the half-oval pattern on the paper.

3 Cut out on the curve and lay on the fabric, matching the creases.

4 With the water-soluble marker, place dots on the fabric that correspond with the numbers on a clock (12 o'clock, 1 o'clock, and so on).

5 Cut 4 green bias tape pieces 3½" (9cm) long. Pin one each at 1, 5, 7 and 11 o'clock, using the photo on page 68 as a guide. You can press these pieces (stems) so they curve slightly. The raw edges will be covered by the bias oval and the flowers, so be sure to place the strip just beyond the oval marks. Stitch in place.

6 Pin the green bias tape around the oval, starting and stopping at 12 o'clock. (The raw edges will be covered later.)

7 Remove the marker dots with a wet cotton swab. Press the binding flat, then stitch on either side, starting with the outside edge.

Put the Top Together

1 Stitch a purple square to each side of the short border strip. Press the seam allowance toward the purple square.

2 Stitch the long border strips to the sides of the quilt center. Press the seam allowance toward the borders.

3 Stitch the top and bottom strips to the quilt center, matching seams at the borders.

Create the Flowers

1 Trace the patterns for the small flower, leaf and calyx onto the template plastic with the permanent marker pen. If you are not using a lace doily for the center flower, trace that pattern as well.

2 Using the templates, trace the shapes onto the interfacing, leaving about 1" (25mm) between each piece. Roughly cut around each piece.

3 Cut pieces of fabric roughly the same size as the flowers. Place the interfacing on top of the right side of the fabric. Sew, using a short stitch length, just outside the traced line.

4 Cut around each shape, leaving a ⅛" (3mm) allowance. Cut a small slit in the center of the interfacing. Carefully turn each piece right side out, gently pushing the seams out with the point turner. **Note:** An optional step is to insert batting—cut in the same shape as the desired flower, only a bit smaller—through the slit in the interfacing.

5 Referring to the photo on page 68, place the shapes on the quilt. (Be sure to remember your seam allowances when centering the flowers on the corner squares.) Sew the flowers and leaves onto the quilt using a small blind hem or zigzag stitch. Attach each calyx in the same way, but leave the top

6 Using the yo-yo pattern or maker, make 10 yo-yos (see sidebar). Top each yo-yo with a button and sew both onto the flowers in one step.

7 If you choose not to use a doily center, you can either substitute with a large flower (see pattern on page 125) topped with a small flower, yo-yo and button, or make and arrange 7 more button-topped yo-yos to mimic the doily shown.

8 Add buttons to the border.

Finish Your Quilt

1 Layer the backing piece (wrong side up), the batting (cut slightly larger than the top piece, to account for shrinkage from quilting), and the quilt top (right side up). Pin or baste the layers together and quilt and bind as desired.

2 If you are using a doily in the center, hand-stitch it to the center of the quilt, and carefully sew a button in the center. You can knot it on top and hide the knot under the doily.

3 Attach a sleeve or rings so that you can hang the quilt.

portion open, and start and end stitching slightly down from each corner so that you can insert the button "bud." Once the machine stitching is done, insert the button, sew through the holes in the button, and then use a small whip stitch to snug the corners of the calyx next to the button. **Note:** If you are using a doily as your center flower, this will be attached after you quilt your piece.

HOW TO MAKE A YO-YO

1. Decide how large you want your yo-yos to be and make a circular template (using plastic or cardboard) twice that size plus about ½" (13mm).

2. Place the template on the right side of your fabric and trace around it lightly with a pencil or chalk marker. Leave about ½" (13mm) between circles.

3. Cut out the circles about ¼" (6mm) past the line.

4. Thread a hand-sewing needle with quilting thread. If you use regular thread, sew with two strands.

5. Knot the end of the thread and bring it up from the reverse side while folding under the circle on the line. The needle and thread should pass through both layers to create a seam allowance.

6. Continue sewing around the circle, making your stitches consistent in size and folding under the seam

allowance as you go. Small stitches create a large center hole; large ones create a small center hole.

7. When you reach the starting point, tug on the thread to gather the circle into a rosette. Leave a hole in the middle of the yo-yo.

8. Distribute the gathers and secure the thread with a few backstitches, then make a knot for extra security.

9. Trim excess thread, re-knot and make another yo-yo.

Note: If you find that you don't need the marked line to turn the circles under for sewing, try using a rotary cutter for the circles. But, be sure to use a special rotary template to help keep your fingers away from the blade.

If you're looking for an easier method for making yo-yos, try Clover Needlecraft's "Quick" yo-yo maker (see Resources on page 126).

Vintage Photo Doorknob Hangers

Old photos and stereoviews are readily available at antique malls; they make beautiful doorknob hangers.
Look for studio portraits—usually about 4¼" × 6½" (11cm × 17cm)—of individuals or families that show the studio name
and city at the bottom of the card. Often the lettering is ornate and creates a decorative element that adds to the overall
impact of the finished piece. Wedding portraits and photos of babies in christening gowns make unique bridal or
baby shower gifts or package tie-ons. Stereoviews are 4" × 7" (10cm × 18cm) cards printed with double images of a given
subject. They were viewed through stereopticons, hand-held devices much like today's View-Master, that produced a
three-dimensional effect. Stereoviews offer a wide range of options for using buttons and decorative elements.

Contributed by Nancy Breen

1 Pick out the buttons you want to use for your doorknob hanger. Have fun playing with your buttons, trying different styles, sizes and colors to see what works best. Study the subject(s) of the photo or stereoview for suggestions for buttons and trims you might want to use.

2 Select 2 buttons with shanks for the top corners of the stereoview or photo. Using an awl, pierce holes in each top corner big enough for the button shanks to pass through. These buttons will be used to hold the ribbon for hanging.

3 Using matte gel medium or white glue, apply any trims you'll be using to the stereoview or photo. These can include new or vintage lace and ribbon, bits of fabric, paper scraps, charms, and text from old books. Old coins, keys and watch parts are also effective (use E-6000 glue to adhere these heavier pieces).

4 With the exception of those to be used for the top corners, affix the buttons with E-6000. If your buttons have shanks that you don't want to remove, simply punch a hole in the card with the awl before gluing the button into place.

5 When the glue is dry and all the trims and buttons are secure, insert the two top-corner buttons through the holes. Thread each end of the length of narrow ribbon through the buttons so the ribbon stretches across the back of the photo or stereoview. Bring the ends of the ribbon to the center and tie into a bow, adjusting the length according to how low you want the stereoview or photo to hang.

WHAT YOU'LL NEED

Buttons
(size, number and style depend on the photo or stereoview you're using)

1 stereoview or old studio photo card

Bits of lace, ribbon and other trims as desired

12" (30cm) narrow ribbon
(white was used in these examples)

Matte gel medium or white craft glue

E-6000 glue

Small awl

STEREOVIEW SCENES

Although most cards featured scenes from foreign lands and popular American destinations, many depicted comic or generic scenes of everyday life (such as the wedding in the background doorhanger on page 72). These "everyday" cards are the least expensive, available for as little as one dollar because they're not as desirable as scenes showing famous places or people. Pick images that appeal to you or that stir your imagination.

Love-Note Mini Pillows

These little pillows are great projects for those of us who save our scraps. The measurements given can be subdivided to make use of smaller strips, and they can vary in width as well as height. The cute pocket on the back is perfect for a note of love or encouragement for your sweetie, a pretty way to give cash or a gift card to a friend, or even a colorful vehicle for a child's exchange with the tooth fairy.

1 Choose 4 of the 4" x 4" (10cm x 10cm) fabric scraps. Sew 2 squares right sides together, using a ¼" (6mm) seam allowance. Repeat with the remaining 2 squares. Press the seams open. Place the 2 sets right sides together, matching the center seams, and sew together using a ¼" (6mm) seam allowance. Press the seams open. The resulting 4-patch square will measure 7½" x 7½" (19cm x 19cm).

2 Trace a heart template (either the pointed or rounded heart) onto the back of the 4-patch square, turning it slightly off center. Be careful that a seam does not cross through the point or the "V" of the heart (see figure 1 on page 76).

WHAT YOU'LL NEED

Assorted buttons

Pointed or rounded heart pillow pattern
(page 121)

Rounded pocket pattern
(page 121) (optional)

Fabric scraps for the front:
5 in coordinating prints, 4" x 4"
(10cm x 10cm) each

Fabric scrap for the back:
at least 7½" x 7½" (19cm x 19cm)

Assorted trims
(optional)

Fiberfill

Coordinating thread

Point turner

Basic sewing supplies
(including machine)

3 Embellish the right side of the 4-patch heart area with trims (if desired). Do not add the buttons yet.

4 For the small heart pocket, trace the pocket template on the last 4" x 4" (10cm x 10cm) square. Using short stitches—about 15 per inch (25mm)—stitch on the stitching line marked on the template around the outside edge of the pocket. This will help the fabric roll to the wrong side of the fabric. Press the seam allowance to the wrong side. For the large heart pocket, no template is needed; simply double-turn the edges of the 4" x 4" (10cm x 10cm) square and cover with trim.

5 Fold the top edge of the pocket so that the raw edge meets the line. Press. Fold once more on the line. Press again and topstitch, using about 10 stitches per inch (25mm). Stitch the pocket to the backing fabric, near the center, topstitching around the outer edge. Be careful *not* to stitch the pocket closed!

6 With right sides together, pin the backing fabric to the front (4-patch) fabric, centering the pocket as much as possible and making sure that the open end is facing up. Use short stitches—about 15 per inch (25mm)—to stitch on the line of the heart, leaving an opening on one side for turning the heart right side out. Reinforce the "V" by stitching a second time in this area. Trim around the heart, leaving a scant ¼" (6mm) allowance. Clip curves, as well as into the "V" and across the bottom point.

7 Turn the heart right side out. Use a point turner to crease the seams and push out the point. Press if desired.

8 Add the buttons at this point, working through the opening to sew or tie them on, or gluing them in place if you wish.

9 Stuff the heart with fiberfill and slip-stitch the opening closed.

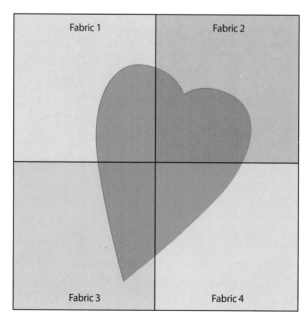

Fabric 1

Fabric 2

Fabric 3

Fabric 4

Figure 1

Sweetheart Swag and Pillow

A small pillow or two (shown on page 78) will make a lovely accessory for your bedding ensemble. The swag can be hung at the foot or head of your bed for a unique accent. Although felted wool is not used in this project, it would make a great option because it comes in so many wonderful colors and weights. Choose warm tones, add a lace appliqué as a base for some standout buttons, and string wooden spools between the hearts on the swag for a country-cabin look. Or try bright colors, realistic plastic buttons snd fun fibers to create a playful accent for a child's room.

1 Trace the patterns provided onto the tracing paper and pin onto the fabric. Cut out all of the heart fronts, backs and overlays.

2 For the pillow and center swag heart, place a small piece of fusible web on the back of the overlay piece. This step is meant to tack the overlay in place until it can be embellished and stitched, so a small piece of fusible web in the center will do the trick. Fuse the overlay to the heart front. Embellish the fronts as desired, using the photos as a guide. Add the buttons in this step, but be careful to allow room for the presser foot around the seam allowance, which will be ¼" (6mm). **Note:** These hearts will be turned right side out through a slit cut in their backs after the hearts have been stitched together. The slits will then be covered with embellishments.

3 Embellish the fronts of the 2 end swag hearts as desired. I used a square of fusible web to attach the teal squares before attaching the buttons with pearls.

4   For each end swag heart, cut a piece of perle cotton about 2" (5cm) long. Fold this thread in half and place it inside the heart with the ends in the seam line area, just below the curve at the top of the heart. A tiny dab of fabric or basting glue will help keep them in place while you're stitching. Do this to each side, forming the loops through which the ribbon will be strung when the hearts are turned right side out.

5   For all hearts: place the fronts to the backs, right sides together, and stitch around each heart with a ¼" (6mm) seam allowance. Carefully snip a very small slit in the center back of each heart, taking care to separate the two layers before doing so. Turn each heart right side out through the slit and use a point turner to push out all the seams and points.

6   Stuff the hearts with fiberfill.

7   Place a small strip of fusible web inside the slit and position it just under the slit. Hold (or pin) the slit together and tap the iron to the fabric to seal the slit shut. Place an appliqué or bit of trim over the slit and fuse it into place with another bit of fusible web.

8   Use the ribbon to link through the thread loops on the swag. The distance between the hearts is your choice; my ribbons are 12" (30cm) long. Fold the ends so they meet in the middle and stitch them in place with a button on top.

The heart backs, simply dressed with lace appliqués.

Silk-and-Suede Pillow

Remembrances of our past needn't look like antiques. This accent pillow pairs current fashion fabrics with your favorite buttons. Now you can display your treasures where you'll truly enjoy them everyday, styled to suit whatever décor you choose. Incorporate silk ties, as I did, as a nod to Grampa, or include other cherished fabrics as fond reminders of someone you love.

1 From the Ultrasuede, cut 1 piece 15" x 15" (38cm x 38cm) and 2 pieces 15" x 11" (38cm x 28cm).

2 For the pillow back, turn under (to the wrong side) 1 longer edge of each 15" x 11" (38cm x 28cm) piece and fuse (or stitch) a 1" (25mm) hem in place. These hems will overlap at the center back of the pillow.

3 With right sides up, overlap the hems by 5" (13cm) and pin the overlap area together. Your back piece should now measure 15" x 15" (38cm x 38cm). Baste ¼" (6mm) from the raw edge to hold the overlap together.

4 If you're using ties (as I did here, for the paisley), open the ties by removing the stitching on the back, and remove the inner lining. Press flat. The silk will be easier to cut if you iron the fusible web to it first. Remove the paper backing from 1 side and position the tie on top of the fusible web, making it as flat as possible without distorting the fabric. Then bond the web and the fabric with an iron, according to the manufacturer's instructions. Do this to both ties (or silk fabric pieces, if using those instead). From each bonded piece, cut 3 strips that measure 1" x 15" (25mm x 38cm).

5 Starting 2" (5cm) in from the raw edge, place 3 silk strips vertically on the pillow front, with a 1" (25mm) space between strips. Place a pin at the bottom edge (the one that will not be woven) to keep the strips from shifting.

Pillow back.

WHAT YOU'LL NEED

Assorted buttons
(6 were used for this project)

Pillow form:
14" x 14" (36cm x 36cm)

Men's ties:
2 silk; or 2 pieces of silk fabric, ⅛ yard (11cm) each

Fabric:
Ultrasuede, 60" (152cm) wide, ½ yard (46cm)

Steam-A-Seam fusible web:
2 pieces, 4" x 15" (10cm x 38cm) each; extra if you choose to fuse the hem in back

Coordinating thread

Ruler

Basic sewing supplies
(including machine)

*You must have at least 45" (114cm) of usable fabric width, so 60" (152cm) decorator-weight fabric is recommended.

6 Now lay the 3 horizontal strips over the vertical strips (as shown in the photo on page 80). Starting with the strip closest to the pillow center, weave the overlapping sections, and pull it down to allow for the other 2 strips. Continue weaving the second and third strips, remembering to alternate the weave. Now, starting with the strip closest to the raw edge, measure 2" (5cm) in from the top edge of the pillow and pin the top strip in place. Measure 1" (25mm) away from this strip and position the second strip. Repeat with the third strip. When your strips are aligned, fuse them to the pillow front.

7 I prefer to attach the buttons prior to sewing the pillow pieces together, but the choice is yours. Using a ruler and pins, find the diagonal line that runs through the woven strips. Measure the distance between the centers of the squares and repeat this interval across the diagonal of the pillow, marking each spot with a pin. Sew your buttons in place.

8 With right sides together, pin the front to the back of the pillow, matching the raw edges. Stitch all the way around the pillow, using a ½" (13mm) seam allowance. Trim the corners, turn right side out and insert the pillow form.

Crazy-Patch Pillow

This pillow is made like an old-fashioned crazy quilt, but it gets an update from the tone-on-tone upholstery fabric remnants and trims. This pillow is a fabulous place for your most prized buttons that might be too delicate for other applications. Here I have used mirror-back, twinkle, mother-of-pearl, porcelain and celluloid buttons. Mixing old with new is a great way to bridge the gap between generations.

1 The muslin fabric is the base on which you will assemble the crazy-patch front. Cut it to measure 16" x 20" (41cm x 51cm). Next, lightly trace the pillow size, 12" x 16" (30cm x 41cm), onto the muslin. The easiest way to do this is to measure 2" (5cm) in on all sides. This will roughly indicate the pillow size, but some shrinkage may occur depending on how large or small your patch pieces are. You can trim it to size when the quilting is done.

2 To make the crazy-patch front, start with a 5-sided piece of fabric. Where you begin is up to you. Use a stitch-and-flip method to attach pieces to the sides of your main piece, and keep building outward. Press and pin each piece flat after you flip it. Make the pieces as large or small as you like. Because I used fairly heavy upholstery fabrics, I opted for larger pieces, which also help you finish faster! Build outward until your muslin rectangle is covered beyond the drawn lines. **Note:** For more information on making crazy quilts, see the bibliography on page 126.

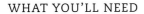

WHAT YOU'LL NEED

Assorted buttons

Pillow form:
12" x 16" (30cm x 41cm)

Assorted fabrics for the patchwork front:
about ½ yard (46cm) total

Fabric for the backing:
¹/₃ yard (30cm)

Muslin:
½ yard (46cm); wash and press to preshrink

Fringe trim for the edging

Assorted trims, appliqués and charms

Coordinating thread

Basic sewing supplies
(including machine)

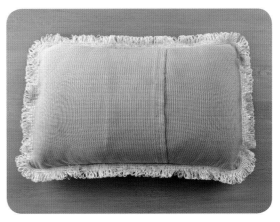

Pillow back.

3 Serge or zigzag stitch the edges to keep them from raveling while you embellish.

4 On the crazy-patch front, sew on your buttons, trims and charms. Try to maintain a safe distance from the outside edge of your piece to allow for the ½" (13mm) seam allowance and the foot on your machine.

5 For the pillow back, cut 2 pieces of fabric to measure 13" x 11" (33cm x 28cm) each.

6 Lay the pieces so that the 13" (33cm) sides overlap each other in the center. The 2 edges that overlap are the ones you will hem. To make the hems, press ½" (13mm) to the wrong side. Turn a second ½" (13mm) and press again. Pin and stitch the hem in place. Do this to both pieces.

7 Overlap the hemmed edges by 3" (8cm) to form a rectangle that measures 13" x 17" (33cm x 43cm).

8 Pin the overlapped edges together and baste. Baste the fringe to the right side of the pillow back, remembering the ½" (13mm) seam allowance. Make sure that the fringe part of your trim faces the inside of the pillow and the tape portion is matched to the seam allowance.

9 With the right sides together, securely pin the crazy-patch front to the overlapped back. Be sure no fringe or trim will be caught in the seam. Stitch together using a ½" (13mm) seam allowance. Trim the corners, turn your pillow right side out and insert the pillow form.

Button Arc Table Runner

This understated yet elegant table runner is the perfect stage to show off the lovely treasures in your button box. These black glass buttons have a gold luster that makes them shine like jewels in the gentle sweeping arc that divides the two main fabrics. The exquisite machine quilting was done by my talented friend Sharon Schlotzhauer of Colorado Springs.

Buttons:
12 shank style, medium size

Fabric for the center section:
light and dark prints, ½ yard (46cm) each

Fabric for the backing:
1 yard (91cm)

Fabric for the border and binding:
1½ yards (137cm)

Batting:
72" x 21" (183cm x 53cm)

Trim:
1 yard (91cm) (optional)

Rayon quilting thread

Basic sewing supplies
(including machine)

Center Piece

1 Cut the light and dark print fabrics to measure 11" x 39" (28cm x 99cm).

2 Set the light strip aside. Lay the dark strip, right side up, in front of you. On the long side nearest you, measure 38" (97cm) from the left edge and place a pin. On the opposite side, measure 18" (46cm) from the left edge and place a pin.

3 Draw a curved line onto the dark fabric, connecting the pins on each side and using the photo as a guide. (You might use a large platter to help create a smooth curve.)

4 Stitch along the curved line. Trim about ½" (13mm) beyond the line. Clip to the line. Turn the seam allowance just inside the stitching line to the wrong side. Press.

5 Lay the light strip right side up. On the long side nearest you, measure 18" (46cm) from the right edge and place a pin. On the opposite side, measure 38" (97cm) from the right edge and place a pin.

Finished size: 75" x 31" (191cm x 79cm).

A variegated quilting thread was used to loosely re-create the patterns of leaves on the light fabric and the butterflies on the dark fabric. A straight-line echo was done in the borders using a solid-color matching thread, creating a frame to showcase the center design.

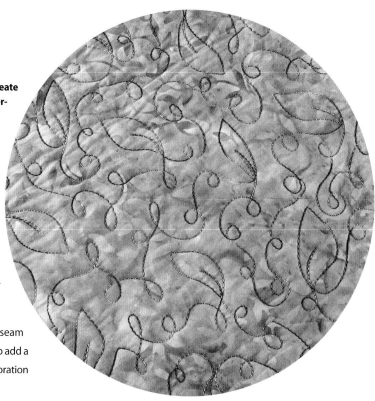

6 Place the dark piece on top of the light piece, matching the pin points. Pin the two pieces together and topstitch close to the curve on the dark fabric. Trim the light fabric from the underside, along the seam allowance of the dark fabric.

7 If desired, stitch the decorative trim over the curved seam line. If you choose not to add the trim, you may want to add a second line of stitching just inside the first for both decoration and added strength.

At this point, the center strip of the table runner should measure 57" x 11" (145cm x 28cm).

Borders

1 Cut 2 strips of border fabric, 11" x 7" (28cm x 18cm) each.

2 Using a ½" (13mm) seam allowance, sew these strips to the short ends of the center piece. Press the seams toward the border.

3 Cut 4 strips of border fabric 4" (10cm) by the width of the fabric (40 to 45 inches [102cm x 114cm]).

4 Sew each set of strips together with a diagonal seam (see sidebar).

5 Using a ½" (13mm) seam, sew one strip set to each of the long sides of the center piece. Press the seams toward the border.

Quilting and Adding Backing, Binding and Buttons

1 Cut the backing fabric in half on the fold line, creating 2 pieces that measure approximately 22" x 36" (56cm x 91cm). Using a ¼" (6mm) seam, sew the shorter sides together to form the backing piece.

2 Layer the backing piece (wrong side up), the batting (cut slightly larger than the top piece), and the runner top (right side up). Pin or baste the layers together and quilt as desired.

FOR MORE ON QUILTING BASICS

My favorite go-to book for quilting basics is *Quilter's Complete Guide* by Marianne Fons and Liz Porter (Oxmoor House, 2001).

3 Trim the runner to measure 69" x 17" (175cm x 43cm).

4 For the binding, cut 4 strips 3" (8cm) by the width of the fabric (40 to 45 inches [102cm x 114cm]). Join all strips with diagonal seams. Check that the seams run all in the same direction.

5 Fold the binding strip in half and press so that the strip is 1½" (4cm) wide.

6 Sew the binding to the outside of the runner, matching the raw edges. Stitch using a scant ½" (13mm) seam allowance, and mitering the corners (see sidebar on page 86). Use the method you are most comfortable with to join the ends of the bias strip.

7 Press from the front so that the border strips cover the raw edges. Fold to the back and hand-stitch in place.

8 Add the buttons along the curve. I chose to hide the knots on the top under the buttons, but I stitched (neatly) through to the back with a thread that did not show on the fabric.

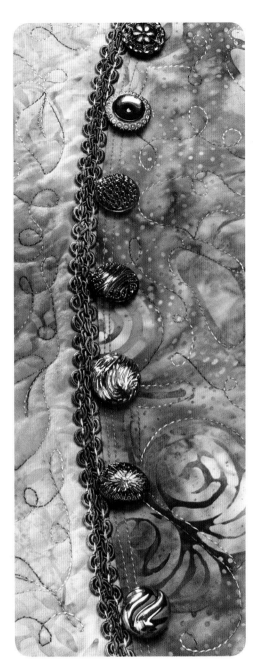

These black glass buttons with a gold-luster decorative finish were manufactured in Germany between 1940 and 1960 and are considered "modern." They have self shanks—molded as part of the button, rather than added or drilled—which help hold the buttons flatter to the project surface.

The backing chosen for this table runner.

Top-Notch Table Topper

Your friends will think you paid a fortune for this custom table skirt with matching valance, but you'll know it was quick and easy! I used matching buttons, but yours certainly do not have to match, or even be the same size. As always, consider your laundering options when selecting the buttons as well as the fabrics for this project (see pages 16-18). The instructions are for a 19" (48cm) round table, but you can adjust them for a larger one.

Skirt Instructions

1 Fold your skirt fabric into quarters. Note that it will *not* be square! One folded side should measure 30" (76cm); the other folded side will be 31½" (80cm).

2 Make a slip knot in one end of the string and place a straight pin in this loop. Pull tight. Push the pin into the corner of the fabric where the folds are; this is the center of your table skirt. Next, measure the string outward from the pin and use a fabric marker to make a mark at 27" (69cm). Starting at one folded side of the fabric, stretch the string taut and, using your fabric marker, mark points as you swing the string to the other side of the fabric. This will give you a quarter-circle shape. Cut through all thicknesses on this line.

Note: You can attach the marker to the string if you like, but it has been my experience that the measurement is never quite precise. You can also open the fabric, after finding the center point, and trace a half-circle or even a full circle if you wish. Also, pinning the fabric layers together along the traced line will result in a more accurate cut. The edge will be hemmed and covered by trim, however, so this will help conceal any minor mistakes.

The trim along the bottom of my table skirt.

3 Hem the edge of the circle, either by serging and turning a hem or by double-turning a regular hem. The measurements allow for a 1" (25mm) total hem, but I would choose the hem width based on the size of the trim you are going to use, if any. The hem width is not crucial to the finished project. **Note:** I found that I needed to use a tear-away stabilizer under my hem when I serged the edge due to the lighter weight of the fabric. I also did not turn up a hem, as the chenille leaf pattern in the fabric was nearly impossible to turn. Instead, I placed the trim over the top of the serged edge to hide the stitching and help it hang nicely.

4 I found that the best method for placing the buttons was to place the topper on the table, centering it as evenly as possible. (Your center point will help with this.) Next, pick a starting point and place a pin in the fabric just at the outside edge of the table. Measure around the edge of the table and place a pin every 9" (23cm).

Attach a button at each pin, making sure that it does not stick up over the table's top edge. To properly place a 1" (25mm) button, for example, bring your needle through the fabric about ⅝" (16mm) to ¾" (19mm) down from the top edge of the table. The size of your buttons, as well as personal preference, will dictate how far down to attach them on your skirt.

5 Sew your buttons on with needle and thread, or use button safety pins. (I do *not* recommend gluing for this project.) In either case you may find it helpful to sew either a small square of medium-weight interfacing, or a plain, flat backer button to the underside of the skirt. This will take any stress off the main button and prevent pulling, tearing or sagging on the front of the table skirt. Sew through the backer button or interfacing at the same time you attach the main button, all in one step. Using a strong thread such as polyester (top-stitch weight) will also make the attachments more secure. Remember not to pull the thread so tightly that the fabric puckers.

Valance Instructions

1 Cut 2 pieces from the valance fabric that measure 13" x 42½" (33cm x 108cm) each.

2 Sew the 2 pieces together, using a ½" (13mm) seam allowance, to form one piece that measures 13" x 85" (33cm x 216cm). Press the seam open.

3 Fold the fabric in half, right sides together, to measure 6½" x 85" (17cm x 216cm).

4 Sew the cut edges along the length, using a ½" (13mm) seam allowance, to form a long tube.

5 Turn the tube right side out. Reach inside the tube and open the seam allowance as you press the seam line flat. Place the seam in the center of the tube and avoid pressing the folded edges, or you will have to try to remove unwanted crease lines later. Once you have pressed the seam open, fold the fabric on the seam line and press again, this time pressing the whole piece. This will give you a crisp edge and the seam will not show at all.

The valance hooks onto the skirt buttons via loops made with perle cotton or thin, decorative cord.

6 Fold to the inside edge of each side a ½" (13mm) hem. Press. Topstitch ¼" (6mm) in from the edge to close the openings.

7 On the folded edge, measure from one end of the valance to the other, placing a pin every 12" (30cm). If you do not come out quite evenly, adjust your starting point slightly, and readjust the pins until they are evenly distributed. There should be a pin at each end, as they will overlap in the back and attach to the same button.

8 At this point, you can choose to make buttonholes on your valance, or, using perle cotton or a thin, decorative cord, attach loops through the back of the valance, coming through the fold edge, forming a loop that fits over your button (test to find the best length) and going back through the folded edge. Bring the needle back through the fabric next to the starting point and tie a knot (I did a square knot) using the cut ends of the loop cord. They will not show to the front, so don't worry about them as long as they are small. Place a drop of seam sealant on each knot so that they do not come undone.

9 Hang the valance on the buttons of the skirt and adjust it to your liking.

Knotty Napkin Rings

These fancy napkin rings use macramé knots and sparkling beads to form a kind of bracelet around your napkins.

They're a unique yet practical way to show off some of your most elegant, one-of-a-kind shank buttons.

1 Cut 2 piece of perle cotton 36" (91cm) long. Loop each thread through the jump ring and place the ring over the pin at the top of your work board (see figure 1). You now have 4 cords to use: the 2 outer cords are your working cords, and the 2 center cords will be worked over. Thread a needle onto the end of each working cord.

2 Refer to figures 2 and 3 to see how to make the square knot used. Make 2 sets of square knots.

3 Thread a bead onto each working thread and make 1 half knot (figure 2 only), catching the beads in the outer loops.

4 Repeat the 2 sets, then 1 half knot with beads until you have 8 bead sets. (You can adjust the size of your napkin ring by adding or subtracting sets.)

5 To make the button loop, make 1 knot set. Fold the center cords back on themselves to form a loop. Work 2 more sets of knots over the 4 cords. Adjust the size of the loop after the first set of knots, then pull the last set very tightly. Place a drop of seam sealant on the back of all the threads that form the loop. Let this dry completely before closely trimming the excess threads.

6 Thread a button onto the jump ring and close. You may want to apply a tiny amount of E-6000 glue to the opening in the ring to keep everything in place.

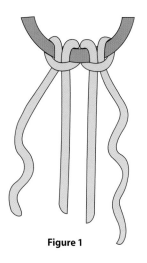

Figure 1

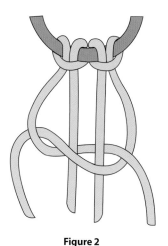

Figure 2

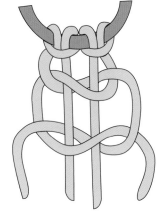

Figure 3

KNOT ANOTHER PROJECT

There's no reason to limit your knot-tying talents to napkin rings alone. Use this same technique to create bracelets, choker necklaces, curtain tie-backs or hair bands. Want a more substantial look? Pair heavier cords with bigger buttons.

Light-Up-My-Life Lamp

Create a warm glow in your craft area or guest room as well as in your heart with this charming button-themed lamp. If you have enough buttons, you can simply fill the jar, but if you use filler material in the middle, you can choose and arrange your favorites to view through the glass.

1 Fill a toilet-paper tube with batting scraps. Spread tacky glue on the outside of the tube and wrap a piece of batting around the outside. Let it dry. Place the batting tube inside the mason jar to check the fit. You may want to add another layer of batting, so long as it fits into the jar, if your button supply is limited. Wrap a piece of paper around the batting, overlapping and gluing the ends together.

2 Place the covered tube in the jar. Fill the space between the jar and the tube with buttons. A small ruler or similar tool can be helpful to move the buttons into place. Fill the bottom first and work your way up the jar in roughly constructed rows. This will help to keep the tube centered.

3 To add the lamp adapter, follow the instructions on the package.

4 Using the pattern and instructions that accompany the lamp shade, cover the shade with fabric.

5 Use the tacky glue to affix the trims to the top and bottom edges of the shade.

6 If desired, add the button fringe by working the thread into the edges of the bottom trim. Thread through a button and tie a knot at the desired length. Work back into the trim and continue to the next point. Secure the ends of the thread with a dab of glue under the trim edge.

All-Buttoned-Up Shower Rings

It's easy to ignore what's behind the curtain when your eyes are drawn to what's on it: a beautiful, yet durable collection of buttons along the top. You can use this same idea to add some pizzazz to curtains or valances in your home as well. Make matching tiebacks for those curtains to complete the look.

General Tips

Some points to consider when choosing buttons for your project:

✣ If your buttons are being used in an area where moisture could be a problem, do not use metal, vegetable ivory or other water-sensitive buttons.

✣ If you have buttons to use that will not fit over the curtain ring's diameter, you could use button safety pins to attach your buttons directly to the curtain, creating the illusion that they've been buttoned on. You could also sew the buttons on, but I would sew the buttons to the rings instead of the curtain so you can launder the curtain without worrying about the buttons.

✣ Your buttons need not match, but stick to a theme, such as size, color or material, to keep your selections cohesive. For variety, you can stack different sew-through buttons over base buttons that are similar in size or color, to make your selections "match." Use a pretty bead on top, and a pony bead or similar-size bead on the back. The ring will need to fit through this bead, so check the fit first, then sew it on vertically to the back, making a shank for your buttons.

Handy Notions Holder

With the dawn of acrylic rulers, many of us no longer use our wooden yardsticks for their noble and intended purpose. Many of my yardsticks have advertising on them that brings back fond memories of my hometown, and I could never part with them. This project is a great way to repurpose these classic tools in conjunction with your buttons and old wooden spools, so you can hang your sewing notions in a convenient location.

The construction method used here by my woodworking brother Jay McDowell makes your holder strong enough to hold almost anything. However, if you're not so handy with power tools and don't know a woodworker who can help, simply attach everything with E-6000 glue—but you'll need to be careful about how much weight your holder can safely support.

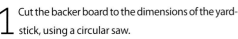

1 Cut the backer board to the dimensions of the yard-stick, using a circular saw.

2 Spread wood glue or hot glue on the backer board and attach the yardstick. Clamp and set this aside to dry while you move on to the next step.

3 Insert a screw into the center hole of each of the spools to be certain they will fit. If they do not fit, you will have to drill the center hole to accommodate the screw. **Safety note:** When drilling holes in the spools, *do not* hold the spools in your hand. Using a drill press is the best route, but if you don't have one, you'll need to block and brace the spool firmly in place. (A clamp or vise will do the job.) Always use protective goggles as well.

4 Using a ½" (13mm) drill bit, drill a hole about halfway into one end of each spool. This is where the hex nut will be inserted over the screw.

5 Unclamp the backer board and yardstick, and decide where you want the spools to be mounted. I used the yard markings on the yardstick.

6 Using a ¼" (6mm) drill bit, center the holes on the width of the yardstick and in the desired positions. Drill through all thicknesses.

7 On the backer board, use a ½" (13mm) drill bit to drill a small impression to allow for the countersunk area of the bolt head to set flush.

8 Insert the bolts into the back of the board. On the front of the yardstick, place a spool over each bolt and secure with a hex nut.

9 Glue the buttons over the spool tops using hot glue or E-6000. Button shanks will set nicely inside the spool holes!

10 Attach the picture-hanging hard-ware to the back of the holder and mount it on your sewing room wall or another desired location.

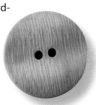

WHAT YOU'LL NEED

Assorted buttons:
7 sew-through or shank style

Wooden yardstick

Wooden plank for backer board:
pine, ½" (13mm) thick*

Wooden spools:
7 small

Screws:
7 countersunk machine, ¼" (6mm), length depen-dent on combined thickness of backer board and yardstick and the length of spools used

Hex nuts:
7, ¼" (6mm)

2 picture hangers

Clamps

Drill

Drill bits:
¼" (6mm) and ½" (13mm)

Drill press or vise

Circular saw

Wood glue or hot glue

E-6000 glue or hot glue

*Pine is an inexpensive and readily available choice to reinforce the yardstick. Another option would be to use a lovely piece of wood, such as oak, and mount the yardstick so that the backer board shows—like mounting a prize fish! You could paint or stain the backer board as desired.

odds and ends

Add a button or two to creatively customize

everything from bookmarks to gift tags.

I love to buy beautiful ribbons, even when I have no idea what to use them for. This project is a great combination of lovely buttons and regal ribbons: a quick and easy gift for you or a friend! These bookmark instructions are for a typical hardcover book, 9½" (24cm) tall. You can easily modify them to fit any book size.

The black bookmark uses two different ribbons; this is my preferred method of construction. The bottom base ribbon can be a plain grosgrain or satin, a little wider than the top accent ribbon. This not only "frames" your top ribbon and buttons, but covers the knots where the buttons are sewn on. The rust-colored velvet bookmark is backed with a same-size ribbon. This type is a little harder to stitch and avoid the buttons, so use a zipper foot.

1 Cut 2 lengths of ribbon 12" (30cm) long. (To determine the length of the ribbon for a different-size book: Measure the height of the book, then add 2" [5cm] for the top and bottom, plus ½" [13mm] more for the seam allowances.) Cut a length of elastic 6" (15cm) long.

2 Sew the buttons to the top accent ribbon. Work in the center 9" (23cm) of the ribbon, leaving room to turn the top and bottom of the ribbon into the book's pages. Try not to pull too tightly when stitching or the ribbon will become distorted.

3 Lay the ribbons right sides together. Sandwich the elastic between the ribbons, matching the raw edges of the ribbon and one end of the elastic. Stitch across, 2 or 3 times for strength, leaving a ¼" (6mm) seam allowance (see figure 1). Pull the ribbons apart to expose the elastic piece. Carefully press the seam flat.

4 With wrong sides together, and seam allowances inside, top stitch the ribbons together along both long sides (see figure 2). *Leave the short end open.* **Hint:** Use double-sided basting tape to hold the ends (seam allowances) in place so that you can stitch them without a pin in the way. It's such a small area to get under the presser foot, and the tape really helps.

WHAT YOU'LL NEED

Assorted buttons

Ribbon:
2 pieces in a width to accommodate your buttons, 12" (30cm) each

Elastic:
no wider than the ribbon, in a coordinating color, ¼ yard (23cm)

Coordinating thread

Sewing supplies:
including machine with zipper foot

Double-sided basting tape
(optional)

5 Form a circle by inserting the loose end of the elastic between the two ribbon pieces, again joining raw edges inside. Top stitch several times to hold the elastic in place (see figure 3). Slide the bookmark onto the book like a rubber band, buttons over the front cover, to mark your place.

stitching should go up to ¼" (6mm) from the top

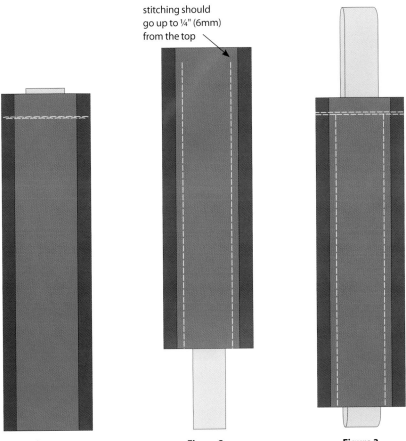

Figure 1   Figure 2   Figure 3

103

Button Baby Dolls

Leave it to a child's imagination to take a fun design and make it better. Elisa, my 12-year-old neighbor, had her button baby doll's outfit all planned out when she crafted her project. She also suggested we give the dolls hair instead of hats. You can use buttons in a hair color (yellow for blonde, brown for brunette, and so on), then add extra strands of embroidery floss on the head in a color to match. Fluff it, braid it, make it long or cut it short. Just listen to your inner child!

1   Cut 2 lengths of floss 20" (51cm) long. Lay them next to each other and fold the length in half. Measure about 1" (25mm) down at the folded end and tie all strands together with an overhand knot. This will form a loop that you can use to attach the doll to a necklace or key ring. You now have four strands to work with.

2   Choose 3 or 4 large buttons to stack in a way that will resemble a hat. Thread pairs of floss strands through separate (and opposite) holes in the hat buttons. Next, choose 3 or 4 slightly smaller buttons to stack for the face and add them below the hat brim.

3   Next comes the body, which you can get very creative with. If your doll will wear a dress, you can start with smaller buttons and graduate to larger ones. Or, you could arrange the buttons to be a skirt and blouse, shorts and T-shirt, or long pants and a long-sleeved shirt. The choice is yours, and button colors as well as sizes will help you define your outfit. Use 10 to 15 buttons for the body of your doll. When you have your stacks the way you would like them, thread them on the floss, but stop when you get to the legs or pants.

4   To add legs, separate each of the double strands into individual strands and thread these through each of the 2 stacks of about 10 buttons that will be the legs or pants. Don't forget to add socks and shoes if you choose. When you get to the bottom of each leg, tie the two strands in a square knot. Place a drop of seam sealant on each knot and let it dry thoroughly. If you wish, you can create a sort of pom-pom by separating the floss and fraying the ends.

5   For the arms, cut 2 lengths of floss 6" (15cm) long. Lay them side by side, insert them between the second and third body buttons, and tie a square knot around the floss in the center of the body. Using 2 strands, thread about 10 buttons on each side to form the arms and hands in the same manner as you did the legs. Tie a square knot at the end, apply seam sealant, and fray the ends if desired.

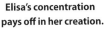

Elisa's concentration pays off in her creation.

Bountiful Button Treasure Box

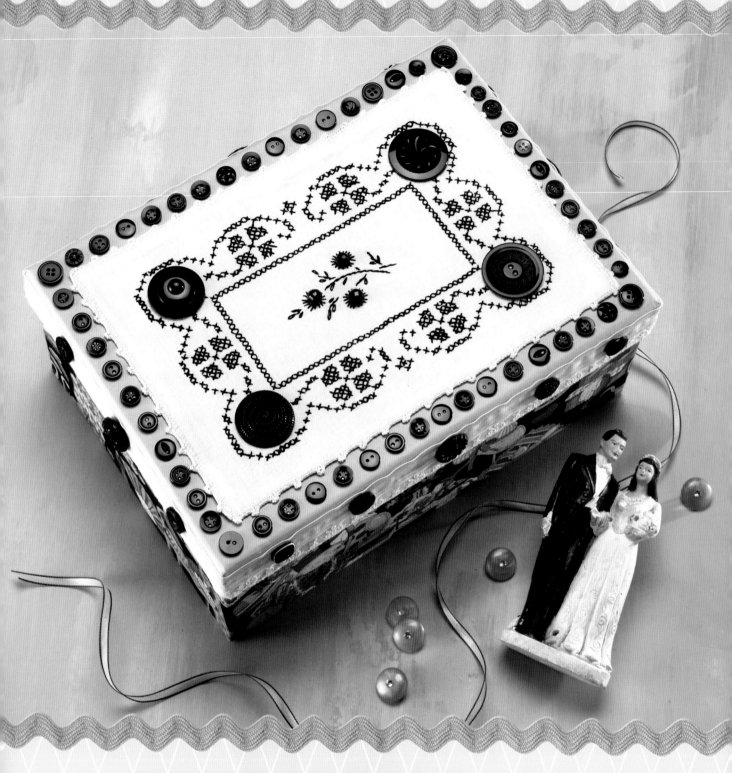

This keepsake box showcases those little black buttons that are so plentiful in our button boxes. Though they may be plain, they pack a punch when grouped together. Consider other colors grouped in this way and you can add interest and texture to any project.

Featured in the center is an embroidered armchair doily that has lost its mate, but items such as a photograph, a greeting card or your child's artwork would work equally well.

Box Body

1. Measure the side depth and the circumference of your box. Trace a strip with the same dimensions onto the paper liner of the Steam-A-Seam. Then measure the bottom of the box and trace that shape onto the paper liner, leaving at least 1" (25mm) between the traced shapes.

2. Cut out the 2 shapes, leaving at least ½" (13mm) allowance on all sides.

3. For each shape, peel off the paper side that does not have the shape traced on it. Place the sticky side on the wrong side of the fabric. **Note:** If you use directional fabrics, take care to place the shapes in a way to best showcase your fabric. The long piece will wrap around the sides of the box, while the rectangle will be on the bottom. There should be ½" (13mm) overlap on all sides.

4. Following the manufacturer's instructions for your fusible web, bond the fusible web to the fabric.

5. Cut out the shapes bonded to the fabric, cutting on the drawn lines.

6. Peel off the remaining paper and position the long piece first. Leave about ½" (13mm) to fold to the inside of the box, as well as ½" (13mm) to the underside of the box. Then, starting at a corner of the box bottom, position the first edge about ½" (13mm) around this corner. This way, the fabric will wrap around the box sides and stop almost at the corner, and the fabric edge will be less likely to lift up or fray than it would

if placed directly on the corner. Once this is in place, follow the fusible web instructions to fuse the box sides, then turn the box on end and fuse the inside and the bottom areas in place.

7. Peel and place the rectangle on the box bottom, covering the ½" (13mm) folded over from the side piece. Fuse in place.

Box Lid

1. For my centerpiece, I cut a piece of fusible web to fit the underside of the doily and fused it to the center of the lid. If you use a different type of centerpiece, you may want to use E-6000 or tacky glue to attach it securely.

2. Use a precut fusible strip to adhere the piece of lace (or trim of your choice) to the edges of the box lid, and then cover the top edge of the trim with a ribbon, also fused on. If you prefer, E-6000 or tacky glue may be used.

3. Lay out your buttons on the box lid in the design you desire. If you select shank buttons as your larger accent buttons (as I did), you may need to remove the shanks in order for them to lie flat on your lid. Consider this carefully when choosing the buttons you use for this project! Avoid using valuable buttons. Use E-6000 glue to attach the buttons. Let it dry overnight before filling your box with treasures.

Flower-Full Yardstick Holder

Nanny always kept a yardstick in her kitchen. It hung on the wall next to the pantry door in a pretty holder similar to this one. I now keep that same yardstick and holder in my kitchen, and I never have to hunt down a tape measure or straightedge when I need one. And who wouldn't love colorful button flowers by the yard?

Cut the Main Pieces

1 From the black felt, cut a piece 36" x 2¾" (91cm x 7cm) for the front, and a piece 39" x 2¾" (99cm x 7cm) for the back.

Construct the Back

1 Measure down 2" (5cm) from the top of the back piece and mark with a pin. Across the top, measure in ¾" (19mm) from each side. Using regular shears, cut a diagonal line on each side between the 2 marks, forming a trapezoid shape (see figure 1).

2 Fold over a generous ½" (13mm) at the top edge and stitch to form a tube to accommodate the ribbon for hanging (see figure 2).

3 Thread the 8" (20cm) length of ribbon through the tube and tie the ends together to form a loop for hanging. Set this piece aside for now.

REPEAT PERFORMER

Like this design, but don't need a yardstick holder? With a few modifications, you can alter it to make a belt, headband or even a guitar strap.

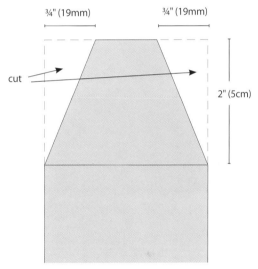

Figure 1

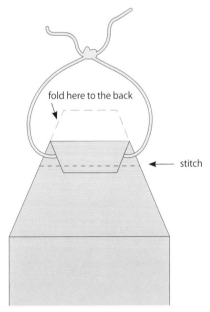

Figure 2

WHAT YOU'LL NEED

Buttons:
25 small in various colors (plastic ones from the 1930s were used for this project)

Flowerpot pattern
(page 121)

Felt:
black, 39" x 6" (99cm x 15cm)

Felt scraps:
white for the flower pot, various colors for the flowers, and 3-4 shades of green for the leaves

Assorted beads:
small, to embellish the buttons

Rickrack:
baby size, 4 yards (366cm)

Perle cotton:
no. 5 (DMC no. 367 green and no. 436 tan were used for this project)

Coordinating thread

Ribbon for hanging:
8" (20cm), plus a scrap for flowerpot (optional)

Basting glue

Pinking shears

Basic sewing supplies
(including machine)

Figure 3

LEGEND

LEAF SHAPES:

— = 1 at 2½" x ¾" (64mm x 19mm)

— = 2 at 2" x ¾" (51mm x 19mm)

— = 5 at 1¾" x ¾" (44mm x 19mm)

— = 5 at 1½" x ¾" (38mm x 19mm)

— = 1 at 1¼" x ¾" (32mm x 19mm)

FLOWER SHAPES:

◯ = 6 at 1¼" (32mm) diameter

◯ = 10 at 1" (25mm) diameter

◯ = 7 at ¾" (19mm) diameter

◯ = 3 at ½" (13mm) diameter

Develop the Front

1 Beginning 3½" (9cm) up from the bottom of the front piece, stitch 4 vertical rows of long backstitches, using the green perle cotton, up the length of the piece (see photo on page 111). The stitches should start close to each other and appear to be growing out of the flowerpot (to be added) at a slight angle, then end no more than ½" (13mm) apart from each other at the top.

2 Using the pattern provided, cut the flowerpot from the white felt. Using basting glue on the back of the piece, position the flowerpot so that it just covers the starting point of your stitches. The bottom of the pot should sit about 1½" (4cm) up from the bottom of the front piece.

3 Using the tan perle cotton, outline the flowerpot. Stitch through both layers to hold the pot in place.

4 If desired, stitch a small piece of ribbon under the flowerpot. The bottom edge of the ribbon should be placed about ½" (13mm) up from the bottom. Embellish with beads, if you'd like.

Cut and Attach the Leaves and Flowers

1 To make the leaves, cut rectangles of green felt with pinking shears. (Refer to the chart at left for suggested amounts and sizes.) Make a diagonal cut on each long side of the rectangle to resemble a triangle. Pink the bottom edge of the triangle, and you have a leaf!

2 To make the flowers, draw circles on the felt with a pen or pencil and then cut them out with pinking shears. (Refer to the chart at left for suggested amounts and sizes.) **Tip:** Use buttons as your circle templates. Another option is to cut a square of the size you want and then cut a circle shape from the square. Your resulting flower shapes should be somewhat primitive looking.

3 Refer to the photos and figure 3 for placement, but make your holder your own! Use a small dab of basting glue to hold the leaf and flower shapes in position while you stitch them in place. Use a strand of embroidery floss to stitch the leaves in place with a leaf stitch (see photo on page 111). Refer to the photo on page 111 for design ideas for the flowers. Stitch the buttons on top of the circles through all layers. Embellish with beads, if you'd like.

Assemble the Layers

1 Stitch a piece of rickrack across the top edge of the front piece, at ¼" (6mm). This edge will be the top of the pocket.

2 Lay the back piece so that the hanging loop touches the table. Lay the front piece on top of the back, right side up, matching the bottom and side edges (see figure 4).

3 Attach the rickrack as you sew ¼" (6mm) in from the outside edge of the entire piece. This will close the hanging loop ends, but do not stitch the pocket at the top of the front piece closed (see figure 5).

4 Pink around the entire outside edge. Insert your yardstick and hang in a handy place.

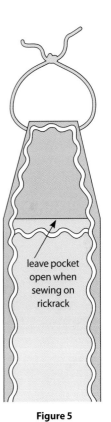

leave pocket open when sewing on rickrack

Figure 5

back piece

front piece

Figure 4

Journal Jacket

A journal is such a wonderful tool for the creative process. I wanted to create a jacket for my journal books that feeds my soul while I write, so I collected scraps of fabrics, trims, buttons and charms that spoke to my senses of touch and sight, as well as a few of my favorite things. Make your jacket your own collection of self—composed of anything that feels and looks special to you—and be inspired!

1 Cut a 13" x 9" (33cm x 23cm) rectangle from the stabilizer.

2 Build a collage of fabric scraps on one side of the rectangle, using freemotion sewing or decorative stitching to apply the fabric as your first layer. Add laces and trims next.

3 Center a ¾"-wide (19mm) ribbon on the rectangle and stitch on both long edges to create a spine. **Note:** The jacket will be folded, with the area to the left of the spine being the back cover and the area to the right being the front. Remember this as you work, because you may want the back cover to remain fairly smooth so it will lie flat on a table, or you may want to put your most special mementos on the front cover.

4 Add any hand-stitched or glued-on embellishments.

5 Turn the jacket over so that the blank side is facing up. Fuse to this the 13" x 9" (33cm x 23cm) rectangle of fabric for the inside lining.

6 Lay your 2 pieces of 4" x 9" (10cm x 23cm) journal sleeve fabric right side up, 1 on each side of the inside lining. Turn a double ¼" (6mm) hem on the 2 ends closest to the spine. This is where your journal will be inserted. Pin the sleeves in place, matching raw edges to the outside edges of the journal.

7 Finish the jacket edges with a binding or satin stitch around the entire perimeter of the cover. I used a felted wool strip so that I didn't need to turn an edge and it could be sewn on in 1 step. Leather, Ultrasuede or ribbon would also work well.

8 If desired, add a tie or closure loop. Insert the journal by folding the jacket so that the outside edges almost touch, and slide the covers of the bound journal into the sleeves.

The back of my journal jacket is just as three-dimensional as the front, but you may prefer yours to be less decorated so that it lies flat.

USING STITCH N SHAPE STABILIZER

Stitch N Shape by Floriani is a sew-in stabilizer that holds its shape when inserted between two layers of fabric. It is available with or without a fusible layer on one or both sides. For this project, any of these will work. If you choose to use the type without a fusible layer, you can spray it with an adhesive to hold your fabrics in place while you stitch them to the product. If you use the fusible type, simply press your pieces (according to the manufacturer's instructions) before stitching.

Button-Topped Tags

Plain manila tags sold in office supply stores aren't very interesting—unless you look at them as canvasses for unique button presentations. These tags have a number of uses. Tie one on a present and actually use it as a tag by writing on the back with decorative ink. Leave one on a co-worker's desk as a thank-you or "thinking of you" memento. Present one as a gift to a fellow button enthusiast. Send one in place of a birthday card. You're sure to come up with more great ideas of your own.

Contributed by Nancy Breen

Basic Instructions

1 Choose the buttons you'll use on the tag. They can be all the same kind or you can group them by theme, color or material (all flowers, all blue or all brass, for example). Decide how many buttons will fit comfortably on the tag and how you'll want to arrange them.

2 Prepare the surface of the tag. Some options include daubing ink from one or more inkpads in colors that complement the buttons you've chosen; covering the tag with scrapbook paper; collaging paper, ribbon and other materials over the face of the tag; coloring the tag with colored pencils or pens; using stickers or rub-ons; or, rubber stamping images onto the tag. Don't be afraid to get creative and combine materials and techniques.

3 Mark where each button will go. With a small awl or push pin, punch holes where the buttons will be threaded onto the card. (For shank buttons, you'll need only one hole; for others, use a minimum of 2 holes per button.) With a needle and thread, stitch the buttons to the card through the holes you punched. For heavier buttons, use something stronger, such as crochet cotton or perle cotton. An alternative is to use thin jewelry wire, especially if the buttons have shanks.

4 Tags usually come with strings that can be fastened through the opening in the top of the tag. However, be creative and go for something with more flair. Use ribbon, various colors of embroidery floss or perle cotton, or yarn with interesting texture. Decorative fibers available in craft and needlework shops are terrific as well, or use jewelry wire.

Design Details

For the Halloween tag:

❉ Spooky images and checkerboard highlights were rubber-stamped in black.

❉ Orange and purple buttons were chosen for their Halloween look.

❉ Perle cotton in orange, gold and black was threaded through the hole at the top.

For the metal button tag:

❉ Several colors of ink were sponged on for a mottled look, then a scrap from an old book page was torn, inked at the edges and glued onto the tag.

❉ All-metal buttons were chosen with an eye toward variety of design.

❉ Thin jewelry wire was used to fasten the buttons to the tag; it was also twisted into the hole at the top, kinked and curled, then fanned out for effect.

For the small blue tag:

❉ Flowered scrapbook paper was used to cover the tag, and the edges were inked with an inkpad.

❉ Two buttons of the same type were chosen to match the color of the paper.

❉ Narrow ribbon was threaded through the hole at the top.

TAG—YOU'RE IT!

Tags come in a variety of sizes. A standard tag (about 2½" x 4¾" [6cm x 12cm]) can hold three to six buttons depending on their sizes, and still have room to show background designs and embellishments. Although manila tags are used for these projects, your local office supply store will offer you many enticing alternatives in various shapes, sizes and colors.

Button-Down and Buckle-Up Magnets

Stacked button magnets are extremely easy to make and can be as unique as you want them to be. Each requires three buttons of graduated sizes, stacked one on top of the other. This is another opportunity to play with your buttons as you experiment with different colors and materials, from china to Bakelite to mother-of-pearl.

Plastic belt buckles can be combined with buttons for knockout magnets; or, glue on a pin back instead of a craft magnet and you'll have an instant brooch. Go vintage, modern or even wild and edgy, depending on the buckles and magnets you have to work with.

Contributed by Nancy Breen

Button-on-Buckle Style

1 Use a belt buckle as the base of your magnet and experiment with buttons you might want to use. You can stack buttons according to size, or glue a variety of colors and sizes all over the buckle. Don't be afraid to experiment, and dare to create out of chaos, making up your magnet (and gluing on buttons) as you go.

2 When you've created your magnet and affixed everything with E-6000 glue, let it dry. Glue small craft magnets to the back or use self-stick magnet strips. **Note:** Depending on the size of the buckle and the magnet pieces, you might need more than 1 magnet on the back so your masterpiece stays where you put it when you try to hang something on the fridge.

Stacked-Button Style

1 It's simple to make several magnets at once. Lay out rows of buttons according to size. Try different arrangements, starting with a medium button positioned over a large button, then a small button as a topper over the medium button. When you create a combination you like, glue the buttons together with E-6000 glue and let it dry.

2 Glue a small craft magnet to the back of the large bottom button. Let the glue dry thoroughly before trying out your magnets on the refrigerator or other metal surface.

Holly-Jolly Ornaments

Make these holiday ornaments as gifts, or deck your own halls with them. They're a good way to use up lots of odd buttons—even those ho-hum shirt buttons. Their simple designs make them a fun addition to any holiday tree, or try hanging them from an evergreen swag or in a window.

Popsicle-Stick Starburst

Contributed by Nancy Breen

1 Start by painting the sticks. The quickest approach is to spread the sticks out on newspaper in a well-ventilated area and spray paint them (4 sticks for each ornament you make). Use several light coats of paint rather than a single heavy coat, and don't overlook the edges. When the sticks are dry, turn them all over and repeat the process. (An alternative is to assemble the starbursts first, then paint them with acrylics or even paint pens. Use these methods if you want to devote more time and attention to colors and effects.)

2 Glue 2 sticks at a time into crosses, or plus signs; wood glue works well, but E-6000 or tacky glue are also fine. Let the glue dry thoroughly.

3 Stack 2 crosses to make each starburst; the legs of 1 cross should run diagonally through the center of the other cross. Glue the 2 crosses together and let the piece dry.

4 Using a craft drill or electric drill with a very small bit, drill a hole near the tip of one leg of each starburst. This hole will be used later for the string to hang the ornament.

5 Sort through your buttons, selecting 8 for the tips of the starburst and 1 for the center. It's fine to try to make the buttons match, but the effect is even more interesting if the buttons are random and mismatched. For the sake of proportion, it's better to use small buttons on the tips and a larger button for the center.

WHAT YOU'LL NEED

Assorted buttons
(8 small and 1 large sew-through style were used for this project)

Craft sticks:
popsicle-style, 4 for each ornament

Paint:
spray enamel or liquid acrylic
(red spray enamel was used for this project)

Paint pens
(optional; gold was used for this project)

Paintbrush
(optional)

Craft string, perle cotton or twine for hanging

Craft drill or electric drill with very small bit

E-6000 or tacky glue

Wood glue
(optional)

MAKE MINI STARBURSTS

Craft stores often carry miniature craft sticks as well as the full-size ones. Use your tiniest buttons to make mini starbursts for package tie-ons.

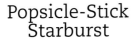

6 Adhere the buttons using E-6000 or tacky glue. (A glue gun may cause the buttons to melt, especially if the buttons are vintage.) Let the glue dry thoroughly.

7 If you wish, you can use a gold paint pen to add simple designs to the legs of the starburst: dots, squiggles, arrows and scrolls. Looser, more scribbled designs give the ornaments more of a folk-art feel.

8 Thread craft string, perle cotton or twine through the hole drilled in the tip of one leg of the starburst. Adjust the length of the string according to how and where you'll be using the ornament.

Button Wreath

Contributed by Rachael Smith

1 Wrap your floral wire around the small jar or glass to form a circle. Bring the ends together and bend them outward toward you. The extra will become the hook for the ornament.

2 Thread the buttons onto the wire until you have enough to form the size of the wreath you want. (This wreath is 2½" [6cm] in diameter.) Twist the ends together securely to close the wreath.

3 Take 1 of the extra ends and bend it into a loop. Twist the end of this piece back onto the wreath where the joint is. You now have a hook for your ornament.

4 Take your ribbon and wrap it around where the hook and wreath join. Wrap a few times to cover up any floral wire that is showing. Bring both pieces of ribbon to the front of your ornament and tie a bow.

WHAT YOU'LL NEED

Buttons:
50-60 sew-through style,
approximately the same size

Floral wire:
22-gauge, 9" (23cm)

Ribbon:
⅜" (10mm) wide, 6" (15cm)

**Small jar or drinking glass
to help form the wire circle**

WHAT YOU'LL NEED

Assorted buttons:
small (3 red and 2 white were used for this project)

Wool felt*:
green, 4" x 4" (10cm x 10cm)

Ribbon:
⅜" (10mm) wide, 6" (15cm)

Coordinating thread

Fiberfill

White paper

Pattern marking pen

Basic sewing supplies
(machine optional)

**Wool felt is stronger and will last longer
than craft felt.*

Button Tree

Contributed by Rachael Smith

1 Fold a piece of plain white paper in half. Draw half of a tree on the folded side of the paper. Cut out on your line and unfold. You now have a symmetrical tree shape.

2 Take your piece of felt and fold it in half. Pin your pattern to the double layer of felt and trace it with your pen. Cut both layers along your traced line.

3 Keeping the tree pieces together, sew along the edges, starting ¼" to ½" (6mm to 13mm) away from the top, down the side and back up to ¼" to ½" (6mm to 13mm) away from the top on the other side. Be sure to leave an opening at the top of the tree so you can stuff it with the fiberfill and add the ribbon loop.

4 Stuff the tree with fiberfill until slightly plump. Do not overstuff. Close up your tree and add the ribbon loop. Start by sewing one end of the ribbon into the tree opening on the left, and continue sewing the tree closed to the right side. Insert the other end of the ribbon on the right side and close the tree up completely.

5 Sew buttons onto the tree in random places. Add as many or as few as you like. Make sure you sew the buttons onto the top layer only, so your stitching won't show on the other side.

patterns

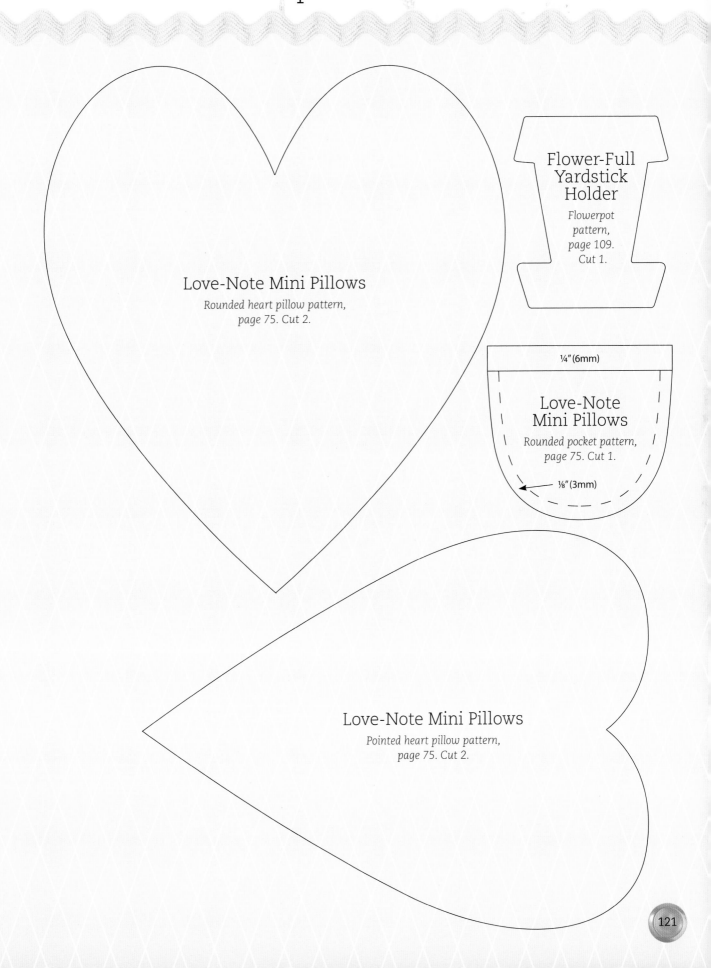

Love-Note Mini Pillows

Rounded heart pillow pattern, page 75. Cut 2.

Flower-Full Yardstick Holder

Flowerpot pattern, page 109. Cut 1.

¼" (6mm)

Love-Note Mini Pillows

Rounded pocket pattern, page 75. Cut 1.

⅛" (3mm)

Love-Note Mini Pillows

Pointed heart pillow pattern, page 75. Cut 2.

batting to here

Button-Adorned Mini Purses

Zippered mini purse pattern, page 33.
Cut 2 from purse fabric. Cut 2 from lining fabric.
Cut 2 from batting.

Sunflower Pin

Small pattern,
page 25. Cut 1.

Sweetheart Swag and Pillow

Swag heart pattern,
page 78. Cut 6.

Sweetheart Swag and Pillow

Swag heart overlay pattern,
page 78. Cut 1.

Sunflower Pin

Large pattern, page 25. Cut 1.

Sweetheart Swag and Pillow

Heart pillow pattern, page 78. Cut 2.

Sweetheart Swag and Pillow

Heart pillow overlay pattern, page 78. Cut 1.

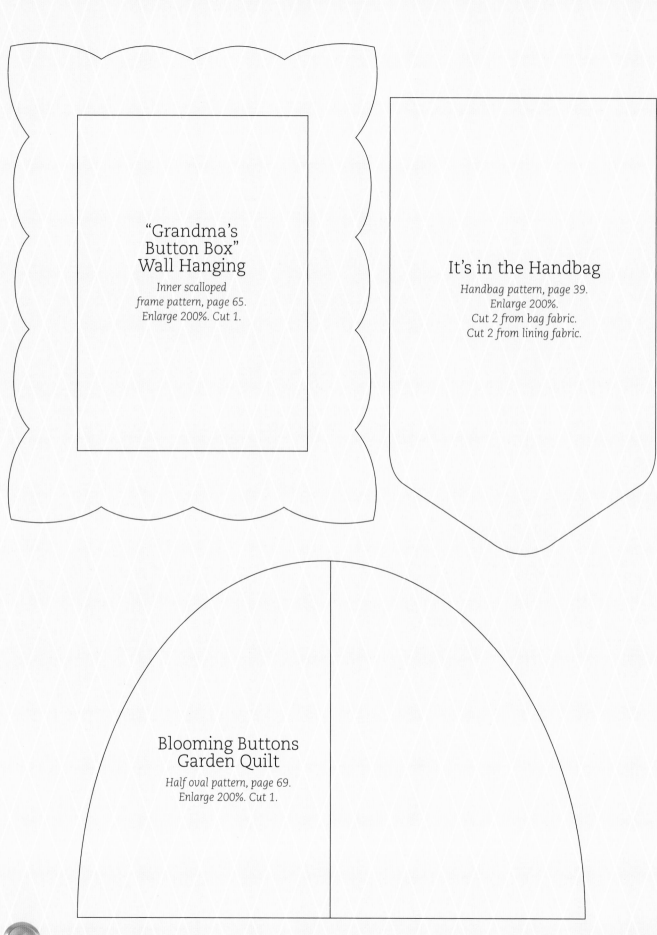

"Grandma's
Button Box"
Wall Hanging

*Inner scalloped
frame pattern, page 65.
Enlarge 200%. Cut 1.*

It's in the Handbag

*Handbag pattern, page 39.
Enlarge 200%.
Cut 2 from bag fabric.
Cut 2 from lining fabric.*

Blooming Buttons
Garden Quilt

*Half oval pattern, page 69.
Enlarge 200%. Cut 1.*

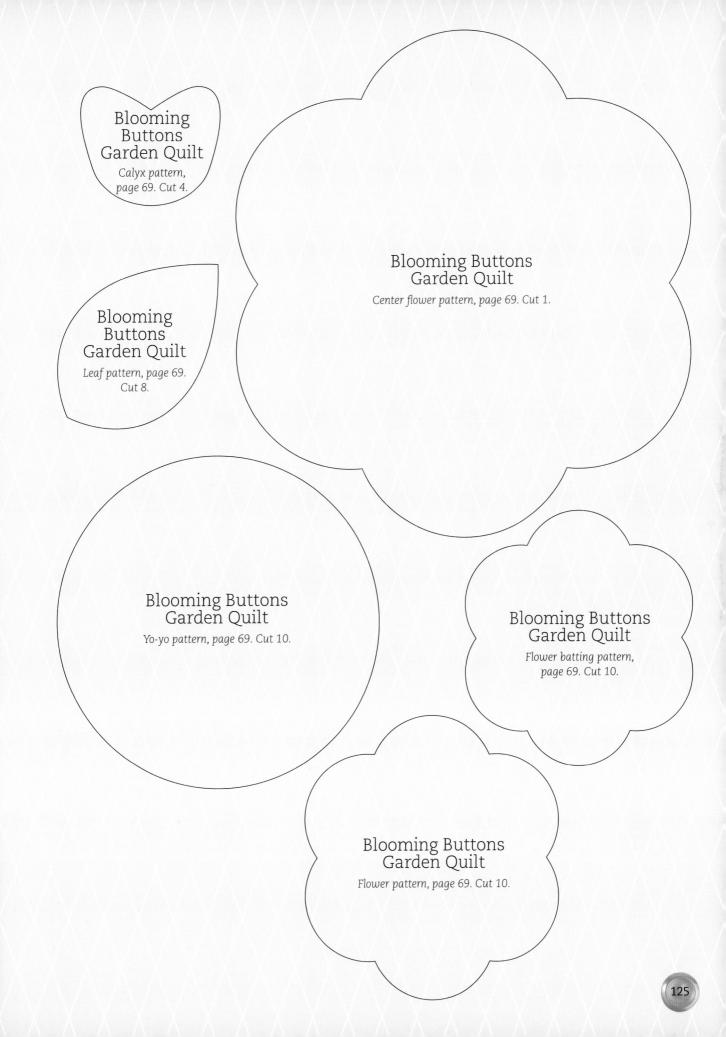

Blooming
Buttons
Garden Quilt

*Calyx pattern,
page 69. Cut 4.*

Blooming
Buttons
Garden Quilt

*Leaf pattern, page 69.
Cut 8.*

Blooming Buttons
Garden Quilt

Center flower pattern, page 69. Cut 1.

Blooming Buttons
Garden Quilt

Yo-yo pattern, page 69. Cut 10.

Blooming Buttons
Garden Quilt

*Flower batting pattern,
page 69. Cut 10.*

Blooming Buttons
Garden Quilt

Flower pattern, page 69. Cut 10.

resources

ONLINE RESOURCES

Jillions of Buttons

jillionsofbuttons.com

Jill's official website, featuring show schedules, class and lecture information, a newsletter sign-up, useful links and an online store carrying buttons, books, project kits and patterns (including Indygo Junction) with button possibilities. Most of the supplies used in this book are also available through this site.

National Button Society

nationalbuttonsociety.org

The official site for button collectors throughout the U.S. and around the world. Learn more about buttons; find your state's button society and local clubs; get NBS publications; obtain button show schedules, plus official NBS classification and guidelines for competition; and find links to other button-related information. Membership to this organization is inexpensive, and the information you'll receive as a member is well worth it.

SUPPLIERS AND MANUFACTURERS

Attic Heirlooms

attic-heirlooms.com

A source for wool fabrics, punch needle supplies, and primitive patterns and stitcheries that lend themselves well to button embellishment.

Bird Brain Designs

birdbraindesigns.net

A source for felted wool and felting and embroidery kits, as well as patterns that are perfect for buttoning.

Clover Needlecraft, Inc.

clover-usa.com

Clover "Quick" yo-yo makers

Eclectic Products, Inc.

eclecticproducts.com

E-6000 glue

Golden Threads

goldenthreads.com

"Whirl" and other stencils

Indygo Junction

indygojunctioninc.com

"Stylish Smock" and other clothing patterns

Prym Consumer USA Inc.

dritz.com

Dritz Fray Check seam sealant

RNK Distributing

rnkdistributing.com

Floriani Stitch N Shape stabilizer

The Warm Company

warmcompany.com

Steam-A-Seam fusible web

bibliography

BOOKS

Gorski, Jill. *Warman's® Buttons Field Guide*. Iola, WI: Krause Publications, 2009.

Hughes, Elizabeth and Marion Lester. *The Big Book of Buttons*. Sedgwick, ME: New Leaf Publishers, 1992.

Montano, Judith Baker. *The Crazy Quilt Handbook, Revised 2nd Edition*. Concord, CA: C&T Publishing, 2001.

Osborne, Peggy Ann. *Button Button: Identification & Price Guide* (2nd rev. ed.). Atglen, PA: Schiffer Publishing, 2000.

Wisniewski, Debra J. *Antique & Collectible Buttons: Identification & Values*. Paducah, KY: Collector Books, 1997.

BOOKLETS/PUBLICATIONS/ARTICLES

Howells, Jocelyn. "National Button Society Beginners' Booklet." National Button Society publication. www.nationalbuttonsociety.org/Beginners_Booklet.html

Schulz, Lisa. "Cleaning and Restoring Buttons." www.buttonimages.com/articles, 2007. "Identifying and Testing Button Materials." www.buttonimages.com/articles, 2000.

Weingarten, Lucille and M.W. Speights. "Modern West German Glass Buttons." National Button Society publication, 2002.

index

Expand your creativity
with these Krause books

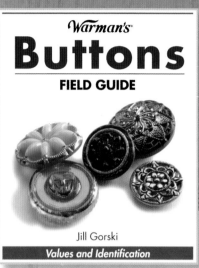

Quilting
The Complete Guide

DARLENE ZIMMERMAN

Everything you need to know to quilt is in this book. More than 350 color photos and illustrations demonstrate the quilt-making process.

ISBN-13: 978-0-89689-410-5
ISBN-10: 0-89689-410-X
Hardcover with concealed spiral
256 pages
Z0320

Warman's®
Buttons Field Guide

Values and Identification

JILL GORSKI

For years buttons have been more than a device that "holds it all together." A popular category of collectible, buttons are a staple on eBay, and a topic discussed by sewing enthusiasts and crafters around the world. This book bears all the color and attitude of a favorite vintage button, with all the historical facts and realized pricing suitable for fans of the one thing that truly makes fashion functional.

ISBN-13: 978-0-89689-808-0
ISBN-10: 0-89689-808-3
Paperback • 512 pages
Z2892

Low-Sew Boutique
*25 Quick & Clever Projects
Using Ready-Mades*

CHERYL WEIDERSPAHN

Transform common place-mats, towels, potholders and rugs into 25+ fashion accessories, such as a backpack, eyeglasses case and purse by following the detailed instructions and illustrations in this unique guide.

ISBN-13: 978-0-89689-434-1
ISBN-10: 0-89689-434-7
Paperback • 128 pages
Z0378

Discover imagination, innovation and inspiration at

mycraftivity.com.
Connect. Create. Explore.